Dark Psychology

The Practical Uses and Best Defenses of Psychological Warfare in Everyday Life

How to Detect and Defend Against Manipulation, Deception, Dark Persuasion, and Covert NLP

Dark Psychology

PUBLISHED BY: James W. Williams

© Copyright 2019 - All rights reserved.

The content contained within this book may not be reproduced, duplicated or transmitted without direct written permission from the author or the publisher.

Under no circumstances will any blame or legal responsibility be held against the publisher, or author, for any damages, reparation, or monetary loss due to the information contained within this book. Either directly or indirectly.

Legal Notice:

This book is copyright protected. This book is only for personal use. You cannot amend, distribute, sell, use, quote or paraphrase any part, or the content within this book, without the consent of the author or publisher.

Disclaimer Notice:

Please note the information contained within this document is for educational and entertainment purposes only. All effort has been executed to present accurate, up to date, and reliable, complete information. No warranties of any kind are declared or implied. Readers acknowledge that the author is not engaging in the rendering of legal, financial, medical or professional advice. The content within this book has been derived from various sources. Please consult a licensed professional before attempting any techniques outlined in this book.

By reading this document, the reader agrees that under no circumstances is the author responsible for any losses, direct or indirect, which are incurred as a result of the use of information contained within this document, including, but not limited to, — errors, omissions, or inaccuracies

James W. Williams

Table of Contents

Your Free Gift 5
Introduction 6
Why I wrote this book 8

PART ONE: FUNDAMENTAL FACTS ABOUT DARK PSYCHOLOGY 12
WHAT IS DARK PSYCHOLOGY? 13
THE EFFECTS AND IMPACT OF DARK PSYCHOLOGY 17
DAY TO DAY EXAMPLES OF DIFFERENT ASPECTS OF DARK PSYCHOLOGY 22
HOW VULNERABLE ARE WE TO DARK PSYCHOLOGY? 27

PART TWO: ANALYZING DARK PSYCHOLOGY 31
MANIPULATION 32
DECEPTION 36
HYPNOSIS 40
PROBLEMATIC BEHAVIOR 44
REVERSE PSYCHOLOGY 48

PART 3: KEY AREAS IN OUR LIVES THAT MAKE US VULNERABLE TO DARK PSYCHOLOGY 50
LOVE AND RELATIONSHIPS 51
BLIND FAITH AND RELIGIOUS BELIEFS 55

SOCIAL CONDITIONING 60
AMBITION AND PERSONAL ASPIRATIONS 65
EMOTIONAL SCARS 70

PART FOUR: RECOGNIZING AND IDENTIFYING YOUR REALITY 75
ACKNOWLEDGING THE LIES WE TELL OURSELVES 76
IGNORE THE LIES THAT OTHERS TELL US 80
DWELLING ON THE PAST 85
BLIND OPTIMISM 90
THE VICIOUS CYCLE 95

PART FIVE: HOW TO BREAK FREE 100
ACCEPT THAT YOU HAVE A PROBLEM 101
ACT QUICKLY 105
GET HELP FAST 109
DON'T COVER UP 113
FORGIVE YOURSELF 117
TRUST YOUR INSTINCTS 121
EMPLOY THE BEST PRACTICES IN ALL YOUR DEALINGS 125

CONCLUSION 128
Thank you 130

Your Free Gift

As a way of saying thanks for your purchase, I want to offer you a free bonus E-book called **Bulletproof Confidence Checklist,** exclusive to the readers of this book.

To get instant access, just go to:

https://theartofmastery.com/confidence/

Inside the book, you will discover:

- Explanations and definitions of shyness, social anxiety, and the psychology behind them
- Simple yet powerful strategies for overcoming social anxiety
- Breakdown of essential traits that make a confident person
- Qualities you must DESTROY if you want to become confident
- Easy techniques to implement TODAY to keep the conversation flowing
- Confidence checklist to ensure you're on the right path toward self-development

Introduction

Do you feel like you are merely a pawn in someone else's deceptive chess game? Are you tired of being manipulated at every turn? Would you like to be able to detect and discern genuine emotions in others, so that you can proactively protect yourself from being emotionally abused and manipulated? Then this resource is the perfect book to empower and transform you! *Dark Psychology: The Practical Uses and Best Defenses of Psychological Warfare in Everyday Life* helps you understand more than just the basics of human behavior. Instead, it takes you on an in-depth journey that explores the darker recesses of the human mind and provides insightful, practical steps on how to strengthen your mental defenses against such negativity.

Inside this book, you will learn the following skills:

- Fundamental facts about dark psychology
- How to recognize and separate truth even when it has been masked masterfully within a web of lies
- Aspects of your daily life that make you vulnerable to the manipulations of others
- A five-step program to help you break free of victimization
- How to protect yourself from the influences of dark psychology

If you or any of your loved ones have suffered emotionally, or if you are currently living through a nightmare that is directly related to the inherent dangers of dark psychology, then this book can illuminate your life! And even if you are simply curious about how dark psychology works and would like to know how to better protect yourself, this book that breaks down this complex phenomenon in the simplest terms.

Dark psychology is not a novel concept, so this book does not herald any ground-breaking discoveries. However, this topic has always been shrouded in hushed tones; there is still so much information out there that has gotten lost in barely understandable psychobabble that leaves you more perplexed than informed.

In sum, this book seeks to demystify dark psychology and equips you with the practical knowledge to protect yourself against it.

So, if you're ready, flip over to the next page and get ready to change your life.

Why I wrote this book

Growing up, we lived next door to this vibrant lady who can only be described as the sweetheart of the neighborhood. It seemed like she always had a smile on her face and a kind word for everyone, whether child or adult. I cannot remember a single encounter with her that was ever in the slightest bit unpleasant. This impression of her transcended more than just my childhood impression of her. In fact, my whole neighborhood collaboratively felt the same way about her.

The only dark clouds I could see around her involved the fact that she was literally alone. She had kids, no boyfriends and not much family. She ran this tiny art and craft store that was pretty popular in the area, and I think she seemed content and happy with her role. When my Nana passed on, this inspirational woman was one of the few neighbors who brought in food every day for more than a week. From that moment on, she was more than just a friendly neighbor: she became family.

Fast forward to 2 years later, when we heard the news that she was getting married soon. My mom and her friends had tried to match her with some of the locals, but nothing worked. So, news of her imminent marriage was very welcome. We didn't know much about her suitor, only that he was fighting on the front lines and was madly in love with her. If it was possible for this sweet woman's smile to become brighter, it certainly did. I remember my mom using the expression, "walking on air" to describe this woman's perpetual mood.

A month or two to the wedding, this inspirational woman put up a for sale sign on her store and her home. She revealed how she and her fiancé were working towards making a down payment for their new home, and they wanted to make sure that everything was put in place before the wedding date. A week before the wedding the house and the store were sold. She wired the money to her fiancé and redirected her focus to finalizing the wedding preparations.

My parents invited her to spend the days leading up to the wedding in our home. It was supposed to be our family's gift to her. Two days before the wedding, her fiancé called, and we all took turns speaking with him. He had a strange accent, but we didn't give it too much thought after she explained that he had spent more than a decade in the Middle East. Apart from the accent, he generally sounded like a good guy. The next day, she tried reaching him to determine his whereabouts, but she was unable to reach him.

She started to worry, but my mom and dad reassured her and told her he was probably on a flight back to the country. She tried to find comfort in their support, but you could tell that she was worried. Every time she tried to smile, she faltered. She clung desperately to the phone: each time it rang, she jumped in fright. By the morning of the wedding, there was still no call from him. What started out as a beautiful day was beginning to look like a nightmare.

My dad kept checking the local stations for any news on a missing flight or maybe a plane crash. Mom was doing all she could to stop the tears. By the time the day was over, the wedding didn't look any different from a funeral. The only thing missing was the dead body. Overnight, this thriving and much-loved businesswoman wound up broke, homeless, and heartbroken. Her crime for the grim punishment was falling in love.

In the days following her no-show wedding, she had a psychological breakdown. She was committed to a psychiatric ward for a few months before she had to be moved to another state to live with a distant relative. I never saw her smile again after this devastation.

As a kid, it was hard to fully understand what had happened. All I heard was that she was a victim of an online scam. But her story left an impression that followed me deep into my adult years. Online scams occur on different levels, but the patterns are fundamentally, the same. The perpetrators concocted a dark and intricate web of deceit that entrapped their victims using all or most of the markers associated with dark psychology. They set the bait, and when the victim bit, they created a false sense of security. This mechanism allows them to further manipulate the victim into doing exactly what they wanted, before they made the final strike.

Despite the reports and general awareness created about online scams, many people still fall victims to crooked fraudsters every day. This scenario encouraged me to think that this type of ruthless behavior is not just indicative of online scams. We also see this coercion in our everyday lives. People in dysfunctional relationships with partners who use them in the most obvious ways, but they continue to stay in those relationships because they seem to be under some kind of spell. We see kids make friends with people who influence them in terrible ways: and despite the solid home training, they make the wrong choices repeatedly. Their parents are helpless and baffled by the power that these so-called friends have over their kids.

We tend to focus more on the terrible actions and consequences than the patterns that play out before these "crimes" occur. This failure to examine the patterns likely explains the increase in victim rates despite the widespread awareness campaigns. In turn, I wrote this book and conducted extensive research based on this reason. I also assessed studies on notorious perpetrators of these crimes, and I made a startling observation. There was one consistent factor in everything. The players changed, the technology was, the times progressed, but the game patterns are almost always the same. Plus, all of these patterns are clearly attributed to dark psychology.

So, to help you and your loved and consequently build a strong mental and emotional defense against such evil influences, this book, *Dark Psychology: The Practical Uses and Best Defenses of Psychological Warfare in Everyday Life* was born.

PART ONE:

FUNDAMENTAL FACTS ABOUT DARK PSYCHOLOGY

James W. Williams

WHAT IS DARK PSYCHOLOGY?

"It cannot be seen, cannot be felt, cannot be heard, cannot be smelt

It hides behind stars and under hills and empty holes it fills

It comes first and follows after. Ends life, kills laughter."

J.R.R Tolkien – The Hobbit

The mind is one of the most complex aspects of human nature. The workings of the mind denote something that has both puzzled and intrigued mankind for as long as we can remember. Philosophers, psychologists, and scientists have sought to unravel the mysteries of the mind. It is a generally held belief that the human mind keenly influences our behavior and actions. Thus, so much research work has gone into understanding the mental process that a person undergoes before taking an action, whether good or bad.

Some attempts at studying the human mind have concentrated efforts on the brain. These studies examine the physical aspects of the brain with a focus on how information is acquired, processed, interpreted, and stored. Essentially, scholars hope to get a better understanding of how the brain can affect a person's way of reasoning. These studies have paved the way for progress in managing debilitating conditions like Alzheimer, perception difficulties, and even memory loss.

The more familiar aspect of the study of the human mind is psychology. At some point in our lives, we have either consulted a psychologist or have likely known someone who had to consult one in order to navigate tougher emotional battles. In reality, life's experiences break us down in ways we often cannot fix on our own. Sometimes, the breakdown is as a result of certain biological markers inherited from our parents. Emotions like depression, anxiety, and fear darken our daily experiences making it difficult to thrive. With a combination of drugs and therapy, we are able to protect ourselves from the internal darkness.

But, what about the darkness in others?

Everyone has the capacity for doing great good. We also possess the ability to do great evil. Beneath emotions like sadness, depression, joy, and happiness is a deep rooted desire that can lead us to deliberately harm others if those urges are not regulated. These darker desires derive from more primitive instincts like our flight or fight response that promotes our survival. Sometimes, there is only one word that qualifies the human response to these dark emotions...evil.

Dark psychology is a study of the human condition in relation to the psychological nature of humans to prey on others. In lay terms, dark psychology explores the aspect of human nature that allows us deliberately and willfully take actions that bring harm to our fellow humans. Mind you, the use of prey in this context does not necessarily translate into the physical harming of a person, although there is a branch of dark psychology that is dedicated entirely to this. In subsequent chapters, we will touch briefly on those areas to obtain a better understanding of the topic.

In movies or books, you may have encountered words or phrases alluding to "a darkness within." Even some of the most famous philosophers made references to this. The revered book of the Christians talks about how "the heart of man is desperately wicked." We have all probably met that one individual who we have described as exceptionally calm or reserved in social settings, only for this same individual to perpetrate an act so devious that we find it difficult to associate that act with this individual in question. Sometimes, we are that individual. As surprising as it may seem, it is not entirely shocking.

Those cases are just triggered responses to external situations. The pot was stirred so to speak and those dark emotions that hid beneath simmered to the surface. Usually they recede once control is exerted. Everyone has a latent tendency to be a bit naughty or just downright evil, if the rights "buttons" are pushed. Some other individuals, on the other hand, are fully in control of these dark emotions. They nurture them, feed them, and when it serves their own purposes, they willfully unleash them at another person's expenses.

Sometimes, these emotions are groomed from an early age. A child learns that if he or she cries in a certain way, the adults in their lives rush to do their bidding. If the parents do not impress upon the child early enough the wrongness of this, the child grows up thinking people in one's lives can be manipulated into doing his or her bidding. The crying would cease to be a weapon, as the child grows, he or she may often continue in manipulative ways. While the child won't resort to tears, he or she will use emotions to blackmail victims. So, what started out as an innocent childish behavior becomes a dark need to control.

The lengths that this individual would go to exert control would define the intensity of one's actions. Dark psychology is all about studying the thought process of a person like this. It seeks to understand the motive behind these actions, the patterns exhibited from before these acts are performed, to after and offers more light on how a person can willfully see those actions to conclusion, knowing the hurt and pain it might cause to another individual. Dark psychology illuminates the dark side of human nature.

James W. Williams

THE EFFECTS AND IMPACT OF DARK PSYCHOLOGY

"When you light a candle, you also cast a shadow."
Ursula K. Le Guin

Given the little we now understand about dark psychology, we know that some of the most shocking criminal offences are rooted in certain personality traits related to dark psychology. But that realization is a broader side effect. I want to bring it closer to home, to you and me. How does this dark psychology affect us…if it even affects us at all? I can assure you that there are no "ifs" to this question, and in a few short moments we will understand how.

The effects of dark psychology are experienced by both the perpetrator and the victim. To recognize the impacts, we need to explore some elements of dark psychology. People who exhibit certain personality traits that are considered dark such as narcissism, psychopathy and Machiavellianism are prone to experiencing difficulties in all aspect of their relationships. If all three traits are present in one person, he or she has a higher propensity to commit a crime. The three personality traits mentioned have specific characteristics that are grouped under them.

Narcissism, for instance, is characterized by a sense of entitlement, feelings of superiority, deep seethed envy of the success of others and exploitative behavior. Psychopathy has an absence of guilt, lack of empathy, destructive impulsive behavior, egocentricity, and inability to accept responsibility as some of the characteristics. Selfishness, ruthlessness, and manipulative behaviors are indicators of Machiavellian traits. Separately, these traits are problematic but combined, they can spell trouble, especially in a person's relationship with others. In the workplace for instance, that person would typically act in these usual ways:

- Underperform in the office, even during the most mundane tasks
- Disrupt workflow due to the inability to get along with others
- Would be intensely disliked by others
- One's impulsivity would facilitate questionable and unethical decisions
- If put in an administrative capacity, he or she would more likely to commit white collar crime

    But it is not just work relationships that suffer. In personal relationships, too, one is bound to encounter the following problems:

- The constant need for attention and validation can be exhausting for one's partner, thus resulting in faster expiration dates on relationships
- One may resort to physical and emotional blackmails in order to manipulate his or her partners
- One may tend to be either verbally, emotionally, or physically abusive with partners or children

    People who enter relationships with these types pay a high emotional cost.

If you have encountered a person whose relationships are characterized by these experiences, for the sake of your sanity and general well-being, steer clear of this individual. If, on the other hand, you are the one who experiences this, seek the psychological help you need to get better. No matter how deep-rooted these problems are, you can improve your behaviors and experiences with the right form of therapy. The first step is recognizing the situation for what it is, acknowledging that you have a problem, and seeking help promptly.

For the rest of us, dealing with people who have the traits I mentioned above leaves us emotionally and mentally drained. Sometimes, the effect can be physical and in extreme cases, fatal. The sweet neighbor whose terrible experience led me on this journey to write this book lost everything physically and financially; her home, business, and finances, but her loss was much deeper and greater. We didn't have a relationship with the perpetrator of the act, but we became victims as well. Our losses were not as monumental as hers, but we experienced loss, too. For starters, we lost our sweet neighbor. She didn't die, but she never recovered from the experience. We lost our ability to trust strangers. Even our relationships with each other seemed to require an additional layer of trust to thrive.

The biggest impact of dark psychology on anyone is that it produces a strong sense of loss. We lose our valuables, we lose relationships, we lose ourselves [I will explain these premises in a bit]. For those who are extremely unfortunate, they lose their lives. All things considered; it is safe to say that the impact of this darkness is profound.

Dark Psychology

According to experts, if a person exhibits one of the dark personality traits, there is a very high tendency that the person will demonstrate the others. In general society, if the larger members of the society show these traits, it is safe to say that the crime perpetration rates in that society would be significantly high. That is not to say that people living in cities or countries with higher crimes are more criminally inclined. There are other contributing factors to consider, but the prospect cannot be entirely ruled out either.

One point that cannot be ruled out though is the ripple effect of actions directly related to or as a result of dark personality traits. There certain destructive behaviors that turn victims into predators as well, and this cycle continue well into the future until someone plucks up the courage and takes the bold step to break free. Children from abusive homes, for instance, more often than not grow up to become abusers. In some cases, in their attempt to break away from their parental mold, they find themselves trapped in equally abusive relationships, even if they are the not the abusers themselves. It is almost as if they have a very strong gravitational pull towards the violent elements that characterized their childhood homes.

For some others, becoming victims can have such a tremendous impact on their psyche that it causes something inside of them to snap. I have read that the "snapping" can be temporary. In a brief moment, they lose all control over their primitive instincts and act purely on the strongest emotion that surfaces which is usually anger. This condition is what causes some people to plead temporary insanity. But there are people who embrace the dark emotions that surface when they "snap." All sense of morality goes out the window. The aftermath of this is usually devastating.

DAY TO DAY EXAMPLES OF DIFFERENT ASPECTS OF DARK PSYCHOLOGY

I am terrified of this dark thing that sleeps in me;
All day, I feel its soft feathery turnings, its malignity.

Sylvia Plath, Ariel

When you think of dark behavior, you may presume that it only applies to any crime that lands you on the front page of the dailies or becomes a feature-length film on the crime channel. In reality, it also includes quite a number of actions that have generally become socially acceptable even if we do not condone such behavior personally. We witness these instances in our homes, schools, offices and thanks to innovative technology, we now see it on the Internet. To help you get a clearer picture and hopefully a deeper understanding of this subject and to tell you how close to home these actions are, I am going to share some of the most sensational crimes stories and the seemingly inconsequential actions the led to a terrible end.

CASE STUDY ONE

News: Brutal Murder of a 14-year-old boy

Traits of the Perpetrator: Controlling, Abusive, Manipulative, Reclusive

Channel: Online Gaming

This case exemplified the tragic story of a young boy from a well-grounded home. He had the same privileges of any teenager in the same age and social group. He had a supportive mom and a dad who strived to provide socioemotionally and financially. His mother took all the necessary precautions a mother would to protect her boy from the invasive world of the Internet. Online gaming was just another hobby that any teenage boy would savor. As long as he didn't spend more than the appropriate time on it, his mother assumed that he should be fine.

But the perpetrator, who was only 4 years older, had sinister plans. By carefully manipulating his young and impressionable victim with lies, he manipulated the boy into visiting him at his place, where he committed the vicious crime. It was one of the most disturbing cases, especially when you consider the age of the victim and the perpetrator. However, regardless of his age, the perpetrator exhibited all the predatory traits linked to dark psychology and snuffed out life just to assert control.

CASE STUDY TWO

News: Worst Domestic Violence Case

Traits of the Perpetrator: Physically Abusive, Manipulative, Controlling

Channel: Relationship

Love indeed is a beautiful thing. When you enter into a relationship with someone, you embark with the hopes that this person will love and care for you. You vow that you will nurture and protect each other. In the modern love language, it is you and the person against the world. Indeed, it started out this way in this relationship. A single mom was working hard to care for and provide for her son when she met this charming man who was basically what she had always prayed for in a man.

He was charming, considerate, and seemed to love her boy just as much as he loved her. In order to fully make himself available for this young family, the man quit his job and devoted himself to caring for her until his true dark nature emerged. Using her love for her family, he manipulated her into isolating herself from those closest to her. He orchestrated the loss of her job, which resulted in the loss of her home. This sinister action ensured that she was entirely dependent on him. He relocated her to his own apartment, where she was constantly subjected to round the clock torture that involved some of the most inhumane treatments.

His careful manipulation of the woman as so effective that when he gave her the option of how she would like to be killed, she actually mulled the thought over because she felt she had no choice and deserved no better. Chance and an act of bravery on her part led to her rescue and incarceration of the perpetrator.

CASE STUDY THREE

News: A prominent Minister of God accused of molesting underage members

Traits of the Perpetrator: Manipulative, controlling, egocentric

Channel: Religion

James W. Williams

There is a sacred relationship between religious leaders and their followers. The leader is meant to be the moral compass that directs the followers in the right way to lead their lives. For years, regardless of religion, leaders have abused their position of power by choosing instead to act out the biblical reference of a proverbial sheep and shepherd role. Except, instead of being shepherds, they choose to be wolves.

Having established his authenticity by claiming to have direct communication with God, this religious leader conned his members with his vision. At some point, he proclaimed himself God and claimed he had a mandate to sleep with 7 virgins who also happened to be minors. He was later charged to court and convicted of the crime.

These three cases here are sensational, but the lesson is what I want to call your attention to. These crimes were not random, spur of the moment type of crimes. They involved careful orchestration that groomed the victims and pulled them in that false state of trust and safety before they struck. As a matter of fact, the way the events played out conjures the role play between a predator and its prey. First, the victim is stalked and observed. Then based on the information obtained during the observation process, the predator makes a move. Only this move is not to strike but to charm their prey and make them feel loved and nurtured. It is like they wear a mask and portray characteristics that they know appeal to their victims.

Gradually, trust is established. The next goal is to get their prey to depend on them. Whether it is financial dependence, emotional dependence or spiritual dependence, the outcome

Dark Psychology

is the same. They want to feel needed. Then they isolate their prey, after which, they strike. It is never like those crimes that you suspect or see coming a mile away. Instead, it is like a song and dance routine that gives the predator the upper hand and leaves the victim vulnerable. In the next chapter, we will discuss just how vulnerable we are.

James W. Williams

HOW VULNERABLE ARE WE TO DARK PSYCHOLOGY?

"To share your weakness is to make yourself vulnerable; To make yourself vulnerable is to show your strength."

Criss Jami

If we examine the case studies used to illustrate the effects of dark psychology in our everyday lives, the question of our vulnerability comes to the forefront. The channels these perpetrators used are somewhat innocent and not exactly what one would classify as a precursor to doom. So, it is safe to say that the premises on which the platforms were used expedited the dreadful final result. In the first case, you have a kid in a gaming chat room for his peers. His passion for the game brought him there, but it was his need to connect with friends that informed his decisions; finally, it was this need that the predator exploited.

In the second case study, again, it was a basic human need to connect with someone on an intimate level that was preyed on, and the victims' emotions were manipulated to alter her reality. From love, she descended into an emotional state of worthlessness, and the perpetrator inflicted further harm on her because of her vulnerable state. In the third case, the victims placed their faith in the wrong deity, even though their intentions were virtuous and very human. The predator presented himself as a vital link to what they desired to attain spiritually, and this desire became the premise for their doom.

Likewise, I have studied other cases following this same pattern. The desires and emotional needs of the victims were twisted and turned against them. This gives credence to the belief that our needs and desires are what make us vulnerable to these predators. Does this line of thought mean we should shut ourselves down emotionally? Let us give this further thought.

We have been groomed to show strength, to not give in and to never let anyone see our fears. In sum, we are been taught that going contrary to these instructions would result in people reading you as weak and vulnerable. Ironically, it is the very thing that separates us from other creatures that have also become the very source of both our strength and weakness. And that thing is our humanity. We are vulnerable simply because we are human. Our desires, our hopes, our aspirations, our quests for living transcendent lives reflect some of the things that make us vulnerable.

But the day we cease to possess any of these things, we cease to be human: and when we are no longer human, we become the thing that we are trying to protect ourselves against becoming. When we stop believing, when we stop caring, or when we stop being vulnerable, we become these seemingly soulless individuals whose sole mission is to satisfy their wanton lusts with ruthlessness regardless who would be hurt in the process. That said, while we acknowledge that our humanity makes us vulnerable, we must not forget that we can also draw strength from it.

This brings me to the biologically ingrained need for humans to connect with others. Recognize that this need is a healthy emotional human need. Without a connection with another human being, we fail to function properly. In fact, I read of a study where test subjects were isolated and studied. Short periods of isolation increased anxiety levels and affected productivity. Long periods of isolation had side effects that were worse. The subjects became depressed and found themselves brooding on dark thoughts for extended periods of time.

Specifically, the subjects' mental health was not the only factor that suffered. Physically, their sleep and eating patterns changed. They lost track of time and gradually lost their grip on reality. They started experiencing early onset paranoia. The conclusion was that we need contact with other humans to thrive. This need to connect with others makes us vulnerable because people have different agendas for establishing connections with others. Some are genuinely looking to build good relations, but others just want to use the people in their lives to obtain some other goal or objective like wealth or influence. For some others, their intentions are even more sinister. The secret to navigating this maze of human agenda is knowledge.

There was a time that the saying "ignorance is bliss" was touted in many circles as a mantra to emphasize the burden of the responsibility that comes with knowledge. I can assure you that the price you pay for ignorance if far greater than burden that knowledge brings. If you want to win this mental warfare against the enticing influences of dark psychology, you need wisdom and the right application of knowledge in what you do. Giving up on having feelings might seem like the ideal solution, but there are recorded cases where this backfired and resulted in even greater losses. Choosing to be distrustful and becoming reclusive made the victims even more vulnerable and susceptible to a vicious predatory attack.

So, instead of shutting down opportunities to build relationships with others, you should stay open but be cautious when it comes to your needs and feelings. I am also aware of cases where the victim's emotional needs overpowered his or her rational thinking. And this is what put the victim in harm's way. Our feelings can act as a navigational system that guides you to your needs, and there are certain feelings that actually act as your biological defenses against threats like the ones we have been talking about. As we explore the subject in detail, you will better understand what those feelings are; as well as how to train yourself to recognize those emotions. Until then, if you are taking anything away from this chapter, it should be the knowledge that yes, you are vulnerable. But, by acknowledging and embracing those vulnerabilities, you can transform your greatest weaknesses into your greatest strength.

James W. Williams

PART TWO:

ANALYZING DARK PSYCHOLOGY

MANIPULATION

"Manipulation fueled with good intent can be a blessing. But when used wickedly, it is the beginning of a magician's karmic calamity."

T. F. Hodge

In plain terms, to manipulate someone is to control or influence that person cleverly or unscrupulously. Like it or not, we have all manipulated a person or a situation for a desirable outcome. It sounds quite dark but let me lighten the mood with a story from my mischievous childhood.

As a child, I had a habit of conveniently falling sick when I didn't want to go to school. Initially, my parents would fawn over me whenever this happened. After two emergency trips to the clinic, my mother suspected my antics. The next few times after that, I wasn't taken to the clinic, but I was allowed to stay home. During one of my tummy episodes, my friends called me excitedly to inform me that a local actor was coming to the school for a visit. I ran to my mother, begging to be taken back to school forgetting that I had "an unbearable tummy ache." My mom told me she wasn't going to take any chances and advised me to remain at home. No amount of begging or pleading could change her mind, not even after I admitted to faking my stomach pains. When I got to school the next day, I was green with envy when my friends showed me all the cool things mister actor brought for them. Suffice it to say, I never faked sickness again to escape school.

This story is just one of many when it comes to the things that we do to manipulate a situation. I still know of many adults who fake a cold to get a day off work. This acting is not entirely bad is it? Sometimes, we have been manipulated into making choices that are beneficial for us. A friend gives you a nice pair of running shoes and a one-month subscription to a local gym, so you know they want you to step up in the fitness department. Ever showed up at a lunch date with a friend only for a prospective date and a sudden emergency for your friend of course) also occurs? I have been there. Interestingly, when we feel threatened, one of the techniques we employ to escape that unpleasant situation, if blunt force is not an option, is also manipulation.

That is to say, the art of manipulation is part of our nature. However, when it comes to psychological manipulation, things get darker and more sinister. In this situation a person's actions or thoughts are influenced with the use of underhanded tactics that are either abusive, deceptive or even both. In this context, the person who is being manipulated isn't given the choice to either accept or reject the will of the manipulator. He or she simply coerced into compliance.

Manipulators have their reasons for doing what they do. Sometimes, it is something as basic as getting financial gains like the fictional soldier who duped my neighbor of all her life savings. In the workplace, these people are committed to furthering their own personal agendas, even if it would mean ramming a few heads against each other. Their principle is very simple; if you want it, you have to reach out and take it. In relationships, it is usually about getting power and staying in control. The need to be in charge fuels everything they do and sometimes they can go extreme lengths to achieve this. And then you have who love to manipulate people for recreational purposes. They are just bored, and they use their manipulative games to pass time. It is crude and vicious, but this mentality reflects their thought processes.

One of the most common tactics employed by manipulators is lying. A master manipulator is skilled in the art of deception. He or she adept at coming up with grand stories that have no real bearings on the truth. Or one goes for subterfuge and lie by omission. Some people are so good at their lies that you almost never realize the lie until it is too late. Another tactic employed by manipulators is guilt tripping and shaming. When confronted for something they have done wrong, they instantly deny it and then promptly turn the tables around by making you feel bad for questioning them in the first place. To further strengthen their hold on their victim, they vilify them thus effectively turning the victim into the abuser. You would find this kind of manipulative technique in domestic cases where the abuser would claim that the victim's character, words, or actions prompted his or her own behavior in the first place.

Other subtle techniques used in manipulation include the use of evasive, non-committal responses to questions asked. Rationalizing actions, if they are caught, and spinning the reality to match their narrative is also common. Some manipulators employ sex and seduction to carry out their devious objectives. When caught with their hands in the proverbial cookie jar, anger and projection of blame are quickly used to manipulate the situation in their favor.

However, manipulators are not always random in their selection of prey. There are specific traits in their victims that attract them, and certain vulnerabilities also make it easier for the manipulator to perpetrate their crimes. Lonely people with poor self-esteem and an eagerness to please are easier to control than the assertive social type. Although, there are people who exhibit characteristics that are similar to the later who end up being manipulated as well. For such people, manipulators study their personality flaws and weaknesses before using it against them. Impressionable people are likely to be fooled by appearances. Brash individuals who tend to make compulsive decisions are more likely to be manipulated into making snap decisions that have long term impact. People who are greedy and materialistic have a higher tendency of being scammed.

DECEPTION

"Just because something isn't a lie, doesn't mean that it isn't deceptive.

A liar knows that he is a liar. But one who speaks mere portions of truth in order to deceive is a craftsman of destruction."

Criss Jami

Deception is defined as the act of hiding the truth, especially to gain an advantage. This may seem like manipulation but, there is a distinct difference. Deception is often employed in the act of manipulation and is one of the many layers in a manipulator's scheme. The goal of deception is to fool and trick the other party. While manipulation is much deeper than that: it does not negate the adverse effects of deception. A lie may take a long time before it is uncovered, but when it is, the damage and destruction it leaves behind in its wake can be devastating.

I know the story of a man who had been married for over 25years. That marriage produced 3 children between the ages of 11 and 17. All was rosy for the family. The kids went to the best schools and enjoyed the luxuries of life thanks to the wealth obtained through years of hard and resilience by the man. He spoiled his children by ensuring that whatever they needed, he provided. And who could blame him? For the first 7 years of their marriage, the couple was unable to conceive. They sought the help of specialists, spiritualists, and even tried a few unorthodox practices all to no avail. At a point in the marriage when things were at an all-time low, his wife got pregnant. He was overjoyed. When the couple added two more children to the family, it felt as though life could not get any better, but it did.

His wealth grew exponentially, and the timing was perfect. One day, the couple got a call that their eldest was involved in an accident. A lifesaving operation that involved the donation of an organ was required. In the process of donating his organ to save his child, he got to uncover the terrible secret his wife had kept for many years. The child was not his. In fact, none of the children were his. Broken, hurt, and ashamed, he took his own life, but not without cutting off his wife and children from his wealth. This deception started out as a lie to one person, but at the end of the day, 5 people (including the deceiver) were affected by it. Besides, the pain experienced by the extended family, friends, and colleagues also impacted others.

In another situation, a young startup firm recruited the services of an accountant to handle their financial affairs. The owner of the startup quickly grew fond of this young accountant. It was a strictly business relationship, but there was a sense of friendship there, too. As the company grew and expanded their operations, the business owner turned most of the administrative responsibilities to the accountant. He proved competent and was entrusted with even more responsibilities. These responsibilities came with many perks and benefits. For a while, life was looking good. But when a failed transaction prompted a quick check on the company's records, the owner was unprepared for the revelation that unfolded. Over the years, he and his company had been systematically robbed to the point where the company's accounts were in the red. The accountant fled and he was left to clean up the mess. Within months, the company folded up. 43 people lost their jobs, the business owner lost all of his investment, and relinquished his ability to trust.

The crude fact about deception is that it is built on the very emotion that is essential for human relationship...trust. For an act of deception to work, a form of relationship has to be established between the deceiver and the victim. The greater the trust, the greater the betrayal. And when there is a deep betrayal, the destructive impact often goes beyond the two individuals involved.

However, deception isn't always something that is done to others. Sometimes, it encompasses the lies we tell ourselves. We justify certain actions with the deep lies we tell ourselves. Just like manipulation, lying is also something that everyone does. Some of us may have developed certain moral principles that make it difficult for us to tell blatant lies or associate with people who do so. But it doesn't stop us from telling lies albeit "little" lies. Knowing the answer to a question but choosing to deny knowledge of it in a bid to preserve one's social grace is a lie.

<u>Let me explain</u>: let's say you witnessed your boss toss your colleague's project [something that he or she worked really hard for] in the trash and you listened as the colleague talked extensively about how horrible he or she thought the idea was. You hum and ham and then you leave the office only to be confronted by the colleague who enquires about the boss' thoughts on the project. Telling the truth in this instance would do more harm than good. And so, you lie. Your intention to deceive your colleague was for his or her own.

In dark psychology, the intent to deceive presents more benefits to the deceiver than it does to the victim. As mentioned earlier, manipulators use deception to strengthen their hold on their victims. For deceivers, the deception gives them an opening into developing a relationship with the victim. The goal is to exploit this relationship for their benefits. One of the most recent forms of deception employed today is deceptive affection. People claiming to feel more love or emotion for you than they actually do.

There are not many things that one can use to describe the feeling of being told that someone loves you. This is especially gratifying for people who have craved this experience. The deceiver gets the benefits of declaring this false affection in the form of trust, sex, and sometimes money.

HYPNOSIS

> *"The scientific dictator of tomorrow will set up his whispering machines, and his subliminal projectors in schools and hospitals (children and the sick are highly suggestible) and in all public places where audiences can be given in a preliminary softening up of suggestibility – increasing oratory or rituals."*

Once upon a time, the idea of hypnosis was relegated to the world of make belief that a person's mind could be controlled by the swinging of an object and the snapping of fingers was considered an incredulous idea. My first encounter with hypnosis was at a magic show. The magician called a member of the audience on stage and then he put "her under." In that state, she did some weird things that I am pretty certain she would have been too mortified to do in her right senses. When he snapped her out of it, she had no idea what had transpired in the last 2 minutes. To acknowledge that someone could have that much power over you and cause you to do things you ordinarily would not do is frightful. So, I understand why we have chosen to deny it.

However, no amount of denial can change the fact that hypnosis is real and is being used much more frequently than we care to admit. In today's modern psychology, hypnotherapy has been effective in the treatment of certain skin conditions and is also used in the management of pain associated with childbirth, dental procedures and even rheumatoid arthritis. While hypnosis is certainly not your average "pat on the cheek and do as I say" type of move, certain people are more susceptible to hypnosis than others. But let's not get ahead of ourselves.

Hypnosis in psychology is described as cooperative interaction in which the participants respond to the suggestions of the hypnotist. That is to say, when a person is hypnotized, his or her actions are heavily guided by the hypnotist. In the movies, we are made to believe that a person under hypnosis becomes sleepy and disoriented. In reality, people react differently under hypnosis, but they are not as incapacitated as they appear. In fact, psychologists refer to this as a state of hyper-awareness. In this state, they experience focused attention, heightened suggestibility and vivid fantasies. People are brought into this state with the use of visualization and verbal repetition.

This tells us that not everyone can be hypnotized [clearly, you need to possess a keen ability to visualize things]. An article I read estimates the percentage of people [adults] who cannot be hypnotized at 10%. That leaves about 90% of us susceptible which is shocking considering how strongly a lot of us feel about hypnotism. I suspect that some of the negative feelings we have about hypnotism is due to wrongly held beliefs about it. Here are some of the more common misconceptions we have:

1. Hypnotism puts you under the complete control of your hypnotist.

In the movies, we are made to believe a person who is down under would have his or her actions controlled by the hypnotist. In reality, this is not true. While hypnosis relies heavily on suggestions, if your mind is not in agreement with those suggestions, you would generally reject it outrightly. So, no. You will not be crawling on all fours and mooing like a cow...not unless you want to do so.

2. You may not be able to snap out of hypnosis.

The mind is more complex than we make it out to be. The same self-protective mechanisms render it almost impossible for your hypnotists to control your actions also keep you alert and if there is any immediate danger, you can snap out of it in a moment's notice.

3. Hypnosis is some kind of dark magic or spiritual event.

Sorry to disappoint you, but this is pure science. It is based on the research work of renowned psychologists like Sigmund Freud. There is a method and process to it, and none of it requires wooden dolls and red candles. All that is needed is your consent.

4. You can be hypnotized against your will.

Again, we have Hollywood to thank for this kind of thinking. A man walks on stage, hypnotizes an entire crowd, and makes them do his bidding? Given what we now know, it's highly unlikely. As I said, they need your consent.

5. Hypnosis can enhance your abilities.

This is somewhat true and false. It depends on what you are looking at. Hypnosis can enhance your memory, but it can also give you false memories or detort that same memory as well. So, the results are really not as great as you would have hoped. It has also been linked with enhancement of performance but doesn't expect to be running the 5k marathon overnight.

Now that we have looked objectively at hypnosis or what it is, I can now tell you that at the hands of a psychopath or a person with dark intentions, hypnosis can also be dangerous. Hypnosis doesn't always involve you going into a trancelike state for it to be effective. The key elements in hypnosis are the power of suggestion and the repetitive use of words that resonates deeply with the victim. Politicians, for example, exploit this in their campaigns. They use words like change, making a difference and so on. These words trigger a deeper search within one's self and subconsciously, we find ourselves wanting that change.

You have situations where it appears a person is completely enthralled with another. After few suggestive ones from this person, the victim rushes to do his or her bidding. In books, articles and even in true life situations, you often hear or read people's description of a particular relationship as "being under a spell." This notion embodies the power of hypnosis. This hypnosis here is not referring to the kind conducted on the shrink's couch. This is more intimate, and the resultant effect can be just as devastating. Fathers have abandoned their children and given their entire wealth to a complete stranger because of this.

PROBLEMATIC BEHAVIOR

> *"Technological progress is like an axe in the hands of a pathological criminal."*
>
> **Albert Einstein**

The subject of criminal behavior is not our focus for this book, but it cannot be neglected because it constitutes an aspect of dark psychology. Profilers, criminologists, and law enforcement agencies benefit immensely from the study of criminal behavior. In psychology, the term criminal behavior is not often thrown around because the general consensus is that crime is a behavior. However, crime engagement does not necessarily make one a criminal. Of course, there is extensive debate on this type of thinking, but we should leave that for the experts. Our focus here is on the elements that make a person commit a crime.

Specifically, I want us to explore why people employ the use of dark psychology to hurt others. This hurt could be physical or emotional.

But before we go further into this, I call your attention to something important here.

Certain people do things simply because they can. Not because they were propelled by some childhood hurt, a need to perform vengeance for an offence you may or may not have committed. They do it simply because they can. As humans, it is in our nature to try and understand why. We want to make sense of our situation rather than believe that we are just victims of random acts. But we must also be prepared to accept that sometimes, the situation is really just as it appears: a person driven by one's own personal desire to hurt others. If you bought this book seeking to find answers to questions like that, you should also open up yourself to the possibility that this person was just downright evil.

For a person to commit a certain type of offence, there are usually certain displayed characteristics that signify this person's capability of evil. This premise goes beyond judging a book by its cover because prolific criminals are often master of disguises. They charm you right before they disarm you. In our everyday lives, these people mask themselves as one of us by pretending to have your best interests at heart. Given what we now know about manipulation, deception and hypnosis, we are aware that predators are not always strangers. So, how can you spot those things to help you make better choices in relating with people? Within this chapter, I will address 4 traits. As we delve in deeper, we will explore these traits more thoroughly.

1. Family and Friends

You know that saying, show me your friends, and I would tell you who you are? Apart from yourself, examine this person's circles. Does he or she come from a close-knit family? What is one's relationship with his or her family like? Have you met any of one's friends? If this person has no friends at all, it could be a red flag.

2. History

Dark Psychology

We like the idea of a person being completely reformed and, in all honesty, this happens. However, you shouldn't ignore the fact that a person with a bad history has a higher tendency of becoming a repeat offender. If the person was abusive in a previous relationship, there is a possibility that he or she would be the same way with you, unless the person completed or is actively undergoing treatment

3. Problems with control

People who do not have the ability to control themselves in situations that provoke them have a propensity to inflict harm on others. In the same way, people who have a problem relinquishing control can snap and lash out at the nearest victim when they lose it, and that target could be you.

4. Anti-social values

In social settings, monitor their interactions with others. People who are generally disliked by all are typically red flags. They don't have to be liked by all, but if the person is generally obnoxious, rude, and poor at getting along with people, you may have a problem on your hands.

5. Substance abuse

Dependency on any form of drug or alcohol is a clear indicator that this person is struggling with certain issues. The abuse of substance negates one's ability to reason properly and make sound decisions. A person who abuses drugs or alcohol may not be in a position to treat your relationship as a priority in one's lives. And unless this person has a way of supporting that lifestyle, you may end up paying for it directly or indirectly, which can lead to years of abuse and neglect.

These are just pointers to criminal elements in the people we relate with. As with all things human, there are exceptions and there are variables. But the biggest mistake you can make is to see definite pointers and then just rationalize them. We have a tendency to make excuses for others. The first thing we are quick to tell ourselves is that no one is perfect. But that ideology can quickly land us in hot waters. Educate yourself, be aware, and then make informed decisions. These do not guarantee that you would be able to keep these types from hurting and taking advantage of you. But you are able to protect yourself from them 100% better than if you are acting from a place of ignorance.

Some of us are inherently wired to want to fix the people in our lives. We see someone who is obviously broken and think if we love them hard enough, we can bring him or her back from the brink of whatever precipice they are on and begin our journey to a happily ever after. From my personal experiences as well as the shared experience of others, I can confidently tell you that this is highly unlikely to work. The best-case scenario is that you become broken and spend a better part of your life healing from what you could have easily walked away from earlier.

REVERSE PSYCHOLOGY

> *"Sometimes, I push you away*
> *...because I secretly hope that you would pull me closer."*
>
> **Unknown**

Reverse psychology is a more refined form of manipulation. Technically, it is defined as a technique involving the assertion of a belief or behavior that is opposite to the one desired with the expectation that this approach would encourage the subject of the persuasion to do what is actually desired. The major difference between reverse psychology and manipulation is that the person who is being manipulated is given an illusion of choice. He or she is made to believe that one is actually making a free choice, but in reality, he or she has been subtly coerced into doing exactly what the manipulator wants. It's enlightening when you think about the thought process that goes into pulling this off until you find yourself in the same shoes as the victim.

Reverse psychology is a technique usually employed by parents in raising their children. It works well on kids who are considered "resistant" to authority. On the surface, this appears innocent with no obvious harm to the child or their psyche, but it has also been known to backfire. In our day to day activities, we use reverse psychology in our relations with others, and it is not always born from malicious intent. Let me give an example using a wedding planner and his client.

Say this client is adamant on the choices of color to use for the wedding day. There is nothing wrong with that, except that the colors in question come across as complete garish and outlandish especially when compared with the exotic venue for the wedding and the prestigious guests invited. Obviously, the wedding planner cannot tell the client one's color choices are too trashy. Instead what he does is agree with the client and then politely convey a story that hints of a very important guest [who has also been invited for this wedding] who trashed a previous event because of a similar color, but then quickly adds that he is sure they can pull it off somehow. This gives the client and pause. The client then rethinks the choices and voila, the planner gets what he wants in the first place.

Marketers employ this technique in selling their products to consumers as well. They agree with their consumer market on certain decisions and in acknowledging their agreement, so they are able to convince their customers to buy their services. But parents and business owners are not the only ones guilty of using reverse psychology. We use this technique in dating as well. Most relationship experts would tell you that we are conditioned to want what we can't have. So, to make a person like you more or want you more, you make yourself unavailable to this person. It is a paradox really. As with every form of reverse psychology, it can also backfire. Playing hard to get can appeal to the human hunting instincts but unless you plan on being elusive forever, you are going to have to stop "running." When you stop, the hunter recedes, and then you have a stalemate.

PART 3

KEY AREAS IN OUR LIVES THAT MAKE US VULNERABLE TO DARK PSYCHOLOGY

LOVE AND RELATIONSHIPS

Those that go searching for love only manifest their own lovelessness.

And the loveless never find love.

Only the loving find love.

And they never have to seek for it.

D. H. Lawrence

Now that we have gotten the gruesome part of dark psychology out of the way, let us bring things closer to home. Because, let's face it. You've read all that and probably thought to yourself, hey, this advice does not apply to me; I can never be in that situation. Granted, the chances of things getting that gruesome are rather slim. But never make the mistake of assuming you are immune to the powers of dark psychology. Its influence is much closer to you than you think. The most common place where elements of dark psychology manifest is in our love relationships with our significant other.

Love is a universal language. It is a primordial emotion that we all instinctively crave. As humans, we are designed for love. We want to love and feel loved. No one is as happy as a man or a woman who is in love and feel loved in return. Some people mate for procreation purposes. Some people mate in order to negate societal pressure. Some even mate to promote the alliance between powerful families. But, the primary reason for relationships aka getting a mate is love.

Dark Psychology

In essence, it is easy for things to degrade to a point where love is used as a bargaining chip for more power over another individual. And this is where elements of dark psychology come to play.

You have heard of the saying, "use what you have to get what you want." In the business world, that type of thinking comes with the terrain. But in relationships, it is called manipulation. Let's explore this example. A woman knows that her partner finds her sexually alluring and irresistible. Perhaps there has been something she wanted from him for a long time but has failed to obtain his willingness to comply, despite their long, drawn out conversations about it. Let's say that what she has always wanted from him is his physical contribution in doing the house chores.

His obstinate stance prompts her to device a way to make her partner become compliant. She has to do this without coming to him outright and saying something like "vacuum the living room or else there will be no sex tonight." Although that has been known to happen in certain homes, it would surely backfire, especially if you are dealing with people who have a natural dislike for taking instructions from others no matter how well it is phrased. So instead, she bids her time. When she finds him in the middle of doing a random chore, she pounces on him. Giving him sweet accolades and uttering things like how she finds him so [emphasis on the "s"] attractive when he is doing [whatever it is she finds him doing] and then she indulges his sexual craving for her.

The impact of this tactic is even greater if he normally has to "work" to get her this excited. If she does this consistently, he subconsciously gets the message that doing home chores could reward him with having good sex later. Over time, he becomes programmed to doing the chores he would naturally have declined to do because of the sexual motivation his partner offers.

This scenario is seemingly harmless. But if you observe closely, dark psychology was used here. The fella was manipulated into doing things albeit willingly for his partner just for sex. She understood his weakness and played it to her strength to get what she wanted. The good thing is that in this case, everyone goes away happy. Because the woman gets the valuable contribution she needs from her partner and the man gets the sex he craves with the woman he craves. But things are not always this mutually beneficial when dark psychology is involved. This can get really dark for the victim. Let us look at another couple.

I would call this new couple Dave and Maya. Dave and Maya have very contrasting personalities. Dave is a home buddy, and Maya is a vivacious extrovert with lots of friends. On the surface, it would seem that their difference in personalities complimented each other perfectly. This was until Dave felt the need to exert more control over Maya. But he knows (probably because he has already tried) that he can't use outright force to get what he wants. So, he begins a campaign to get Maya under his thumb. He starts by nitpicking little details about her like her choice in clothing, makeup, hair, and even makes snide comments about her weight under the guise of love, of course.

This starts affecting her confidence and when she brings up her friends, he uses flimsy incidents to illustrate and back up his theory about some fictional feud between them [things like they are jealous of you usually works]. These little seeds of doubts grow and fully blossom into a wedge that drives Maya and her friends further apart. With no friends and poor esteem issues thanks to her new-found low confidence, she is made to feel like Dave is the only person who truly cares about her and accepts her for who she is. This drives her to want to do everything she can to please Dave thus putting her exactly where he wants her to be...under his thumb and fully under his control.

In the two cases I used as an illustration, we see instances where relationships that are supposed to be about the two persons involved becomes a channel to fulfill the desires of one partner through manipulation and deception. Both relationships started out with good intentions; a while the end result of the former proved to be a satisfactory situation for both parties, the reverse is the case in the latter. The similarities here are that all victims did what they did out of their feelings for their partners. It therefore goes on to say that our desires to be loved can leave us vulnerable. Love can be manipulated and exploited for others' gains.

James W. Williams

BLIND FAITH AND RELIGIOUS BELIEFS

*"If we seek solace in the prisons of the distant past
Security in human systems we're told will always, always last
Emotions are the sail and blind faith is the mast
Without the breath of real freedom we're getting nowhere fast."*

Sting

I am just going to throw this out there and say that blind faith does not only refer to the belief in one supreme God or higher deity. Some people chose to believe in science. Regardless of what faith you practice, there is a fact that our faith sometimes creates a blind spot that distorts the reality causing us to make decisions that we probably wouldn't if we were in our right and proper state of mind. But before we get into the what, let us look at the why.

When I talked about vulnerability in an earlier chapter, I mentioned that the very things that makes us human are some of the things that makes us vulnerable and susceptible to the machinations of dark psychology. For some people, these influences are evident than others. Our beliefs in deities predate even the earliest civilization. Man has always regarded his existence as a small fraction in the universal scheme of things, so we believe that there are forces that are bigger, greater and divine. If you examined things logically, this kind of thinking made sense because it helped our minds cope with the inexplicable actions that happen all around us.

You see a beautiful flower and marvel at how something so exquisite and delicate could just be...without thought, without pattern, it just is. We look at the big expanse of the sky and wonder what lies beyond. Does it just go on forever? Or does it just tapper off into an endless end? When you hear the powerful roar of the waterfall or the earth-shaking sounds made by a thunder blast, even with the advancements and knowledge made available to us, we still quake in fear and awe. Back then, your choices were to either let the fear drive you insane or you rationalize the situation by pinning it on a sovereign being that is bigger than you. Some of the braver folk chose to use science to validate their explanation.

Staying with this same line of thinking, when someone we love dies, we are forced to confront our own mortality. Our grief is compounded by questions regarding life and death. Does the journey end here or does it continue into the afterlife? This has been a strong motivational force behind today's belief systems. The fear and consideration given to the life after this life has spurred many into making the "right choices" here, so that when death comes, the life that we hope continues after us is favorable for us. It is our own way of manipulating the final outcome so to speak because the alternative as it is been portrayed to us is so grim. Some people prey on our fear of the afterlife, so they use it to manipulate us into getting what they want.

If we hold this afterlife theory in such high esteem, you can imagine how we treat people who are considered mouthpieces of the deities that control the afterlife. Pastors,

Imams, Rabbis, and all other form of religious leaders are held in such high reverence that their words are considered the words of the deity in question. Generally speaking, these religious leaders are meant to apply morally sound principles in accordance with their respective offices and act in the best interest of their members. If not for any other reason, at least to promote the tenets of the faith they claim to represent. However, this is not always the case as we have come to realize. A lot of religious leaders abuse their roles and influence by deceiving their members into making decisions that only serve their selfish agendas.

The common tactic is to use the name of the principal deity to twists the words that are drawn from the religion's sacred manual to mean new things that corroborate whatever story they are making up in order to help them successfully manipulate the people. A lot of people have been swindled, physically hurt and even made to commit atrocious crimes under this guise. Another method these false leaders use is claiming to have a vision or spiritual insight into a specific need that the victim has. They create an elaborate story that is a mishmash of lies interspersed with the truth (usually obtained unknowingly from the victim or third parties) and the main goal is to extort the victim for money, favor or just power play. Some victims are coerced to part with more money than they can ever hope to have. In some cases, young impressionable victims are brainwashed into living in fear under occult-like situations.

But, scenarios like these don't just end in religious houses. There are people who are not affiliated with any religion, but they like to consider themselves spiritually open. Such people would encounter fake psychics and mediums who claim to have a strong connection with the netherworld. Again, our attachment to people who have died, as well as our concerns for what happens after death, clouds our judgments and leaves us open to crooks who would like to manipulate the situation to their advantage. They employ the same trick of the false religious leaders using deception and lies to manipulate their victims. Victims go for a 10-minute psychic reading of their horoscopes and palms only to get strung along for years with promises, altered realities, and false hopes, which cause them to spend thousands and thousands of dollars searching for the elusive "truth."

People who place their hope in science are not immune to manipulations. If you are thinking that because your faith is anchored to legible and factual science, you cannot be influenced, think again. When there is a crisis, people revert to what they believe in. For a science believer, you naturally turn to science. There are cases where people with debilitating medical condition seek out unconventional medicine in a bid to outlive the disease. Knowing that the best of conventional medicine has failed, they turn to these outliers who claim to have the solution with their experimental drugs and never-been-done-before medical procedures. Unfortunately, these procedures are too risky, too expensive, and often uninsured. But the slim chance of life is worth every penny and this is what the fraudulent people exploit.

And it is not just in crisis. You have people come up with wonder solutions to a mass problem like weight loss and so on. They claim that their latest diet fad, wonder pill or technology can transform us using scientific theories that have not been tested and verified. Many people buy into the promise of this transformation based on information that has been specifically manipulated to extort victims. The main difference between religious con leaders and these purveyors of fake science is that instead of a deity, they use science when swindling their victims. And sadly, most people don't realize until is too late just how badly they are being affected.

When it comes to belief, those who use dark psychology key into your deepest needs and exploit it. They use that which you hold sacred to manipulate your thought process. And sometimes, the sacredness of it doesn't really matter. As long as it is important to you, they consider it a gold mine of some sort. And there is no greater time to mine and individual so to speak than when that individual is experiencing a crisis. This is because, in your moment of crisis, you are at your weakest and most susceptible to the influences of others and people have been known to manipulate things to their own advantage.

SOCIAL CONDITIONING

> *Where justice is denied, where poverty is enforced Where ignorance prevails and where any one class is made to feel that the society is an organized conspiracy to oppress, rob and degrade them, neither persons nor property will be safe.*
>
> **Frederick Douglas**

During a group discussion when I was in school, I heard an argument where someone vehemently declared that we are a product of our society. I wanted to dispute that right there because I was privileged to know many successful individuals who defied their society and distinguished themselves by accomplishing very impressive feats. As I grew older and experienced more of life, it dawned on me that these individuals were the "exceptions." It is an undeniable fact that the society we live in plays a tremendous role that shapes us in more ways than we can imagine. The ugly truth is that the way we think, live, and function can be traced to the influences of our society and these are some of the things that dark psychology exploits.

Social conditioning refers to the impact the society has on your life as a whole. While social conditioning looks more at your social status in terms of income, living conditions and so on, its reach can go deeper than that. Your society can and does influence your beliefs and religion. You may not be a direct practitioner of those beliefs, but you are indirectly affected by it. In certain cultures, certain days are considered sacred. That means, conducting business on those days might be considered an offence. But seeing as we have just discussed religion in the previous chapter, let us look at other aspects of social conditioning that can easily be influenced by dark psychology.

There is a general misconception that being part of a society that is more advanced makes you impervious to the influences of culture. I totally get that kind of reasoning. How can a society that gave birth to the likes of Albert Einstein and Neil Armstrong be impacted by something as ridiculous as culture right? Well, you are wrong on that count. If anything, you are even more vulnerable, and I will tell you about it in a bit.

The biggest advancement our society has made today is in the area of technology. We live in a world where things are done in a flash. Money transactions are completed at the push of a button. A businessman can conclude a deal in China, motivate his team in South America, talk his partner through a crisis at home, and deliver an impressive marketing pitch in Dubai all before the morning is done just by pressing a few buttons. This is the world we live in today. If you are coming up with a business plan in this era, your products and services have to match the same speed that we are all used or else you are setting up yourself to fail. And this is very good. Because I am fairly certain that no one misses the good old days when it took one whole month to get a mail from across the country or three puffs of black smoke shooting in the sky to tell you that your beloved loves you back. No. We appreciate the pace with which things are done these days.

Unfortunately, this speed that characterizes our daily lives makes us vulnerable to get rich quick schemes. We hear all these amazing stories of people who became millionaires overnight and on some subconscious level, we desire the same thing. Some people have exploited these desires to their advantage with what we now know as Ponzi schemes. Named after the infamous Charles Ponzi, a Ponzi scheme is a diabolical way of carrying out daytime robbery with full consent from the victim. The scam artists come up with a fictitious enterprise that promises huge returns on investment. After the victim makes an initial commitment, he is rewarded with "returns," which draw in him further into the trap the perpetrators have laid out causing him to put in more funds. To even maximize his profits, the victim is manipulated into bringing in more friends to make investments. The more friends he brings, the higher his returns. This builds a pyramid of investors all pouring their funds into this enterprise that does not exist. In reality, what the scammers are doing is simply robbing Peter to pay Paul. Then they pay themselves as well. This continues until one day; the company just vanishes into thin air leaving lots of victims stranded and without their initial investment or returns on it.

The only logical explanation we can give for a situation like this where a company with barely any registered documentation of its existence comes in and swindles hard working people who are usually smart in their dealings is social conditioning. It happened in the 1800s, in the 1900s, and it is still occurring to this very day. And despite the knowledge of its existence, people are still falling for Ponzi schemes. It is like we are just programmed to do it. Plus, it is not just a restricted to a certain class of people. Both rich people and poor people fall for it. That tells us that the perpetrator preys on something that these two classes of people have in common: is a desire to make more money and to make that money fast.

But it doesn't just end there. To successfully commit this crime, they rely on our sense of community. You are more likely to patronize the services or products of a company if you were given a direct referral by someone you trust that the recommendations of a random stranger. If your sister shows up saying she made xyz amount of money on an investment and she shows you proof of it, instinctively, your trust causes you to base your decision almost entirely on their reference. And when you get your own payout, you automatically become an ambassador for the brand. This makes you spread your own news to other people in your network and the chain continues. This is a very human behavior and a lot of manipulators would capitalize on this. As soon as they get what they need, they disappear or get consumed by their greed and get caught.

You might argue that this scenario is not likely to happen to you because you are just too smart for this, so let me bring it closer to home using technology that we go to bed with and wake up to every day. Social media is the craze of our time. People have become "overnight" sensations thanks to social media platforms like YouTube, Instagram, Twitter, and Facebook among others. This has caused some of us to nurse similar dreams, but until that happens, we are willing to settle for the likes and comments we get. The problem is that our natural desire to connect with people can become somewhat obsessive if the focus is on our virtual relationships on social media. This grows into a disturbing thought process where one's sense of accomplishment is equated with the number of likes, follows, and comments one can get from a post.

Individuals who start thinking in this manner stop paying attention to their actual real-life relationships. Instead, they lead fake and pretentious lives just so that they can get approval that in a sad way validates their daily lives. In their quest for relevance, they starve themselves emotionally and subject themselves to the sometimes cruel and disapproving opinions of others. This sort of behavior has been linked to the increase of suicidal behavior in people who use social media. It is quite ironic that social media, which was designed to help us connect with other people and build our network has broken many people instead due to its dark influences.

James W. Williams

AMBITION AND PERSONAL ASPIRATIONS

Great ambition is the passion of a great character.

Those endowed with it may perform very good or very bad acts.

All depends on the principles which guide them.

Napoleon Bonaparte

We all have a to-do list. Sometimes, this list is just a group of tasks designed to help us get through the day. And sometimes, it is a roadmap to where we would like to be in the nearest future. For example,, your grocery shopping list gets you through the day in that you are able to get what you need to make dinner and possibly the basic essentials that helps you become a better member of the society (ye olde regular bathing soap keeps the bad odors away and the society thanks you for it). But, drawing up a business plan for your startup? That is a different ball game entirely. You are trying to set yourself up for the future financially and quite possibly, providing a product or service that impacts the lives of people positively. In today's terminology, we call that "boss moves."

Ambition is what drives you towards those goals you set for yourself. You want something? You push yourself to attain it and for the more ambitious folks, when they achieve their goals, they simply push themselves some more. Ambition is an attractive trait in any human. The aspiration to be better than who, what and where you are now often puts you at the wheel that steers your life. Nobody wants to be with people who are content to sit on the couch all day doing nothing more than eating potato chips and flipping through channels. People want to be with someone who is truly excited about the beautiful future envisioned and are meticulously working to achieve it.

However, as attractive as ambition is, when it is put in overdrive, it can attract the wrong sort of people into your life because it leaves you open and vulnerable. This may sound like a contradictive statement because ambitious people are described as anything but vulnerable. But, as you will come to learn in this book, what you allow to consume you gains control over you and when you have no control, you become vulnerable. In earlier chapters, I talked about how predators use the weaknesses of their victims against them. Bearing this in mind, you would agree that ambition is an admirable trait in a person. As a strength, it can help you navigate your path to success. But as a weakness, it can very easily be the architect of your destruction.

Where ambition drives your goals, your personal aspirations, on the other hand, can be looked as your success indicators. There many similarities between aspirations and ambitions, but the main difference is the magnitude and intensity of the later. Your ambition could be to climb up the managerial ladder before the year is over, and your aspiration could be to be open up more employment opportunities when you attain that position. Ambition is more concrete in its desires while aspirations are those noble notions that we nurse to make us feel better about ourselves. On their own, neither ambition nor aspirations should bring you harm, but when other elements come into play, they can be used to manipulate and deceive you.

Most organizations believe that ambition is one of the most desirable qualities in a potential employee. Yet this is usually because ambitious people are more willing to do what needs to be done to advance the company than their more seemingly docile counterparts. People like these are very focused and have a one-track mind when it comes to carrying out their responsibilities; sometimes giving no thought to what it would take to do it even if it would mean stepping on the toes of a few colleagues. In certain contexts, this can be good. After all, the workplace and the world in general is not a playground where the rules of equity for all applies. But this attitude can quickly create a hostile work environment that makes it difficult for employees to thrive. The goals of the organization may be met consistently, but at the detriment of its employees. But this is not the immediate danger although, that is not saying that a situation like this is not an issue for concern either.

A person who does not reign in one's ambition can be persuaded and manipulated into doing things that are morally and ethically wrong just to meet his or her goals. People with lofty ambitions and aspirations that are more likely to fall for manipulative techniques that involve blackmail. For instance, a young career man with a sterling reputation and a good position within a company is more likely to do anything to retain that status quo if he is ambitious. Even if those things he is expected to do would further taint his reputation if the knowledge of those deeds ever came to light. This is not to say that the rest of us are less likely to become victims of blackmail and other forms of manipulation.

Manipulation is not about physically wielding a big dangerous axe over a person to force him or her to do something out of the ordinary. It is a game of subterfuge and deception. The manipulator acts like a mirror that captures the desires, ambitions and aspirations of the victim and then threatens the actualization of that vision by also displaying the victim's weakness. The victim is made to falsely believe that one's only hope of salvaging their dreams is to comply with the wishes of the manipulator. The stronger the ambition, the more likely the victim will comply, especially if he or she is convinced that the person can get away with doing it.

The acts they could be manipulated into carrying could be anything from undermining the authority figure in their lives, committing an act that might be offensive or one of any of whatever else the manipulator may have in mind. Let me scale this back to relatable proportions. In all of our relationships with people, there is a measure of trust. No matter how paranoid you may be, even the business relationship you have with your tailor is an indication of some level of trust in that you are trusting in someone to help you cover your nakedness without getting harmed in the process. But in as much as there is trust, there is also distrust. We strive to work through these feelings in the hope of maintaining the bond/bridge between the people involved.

At best, we aspire to maintain civility with those around us. A predator with malicious intent can expound on the distrust by sowing seeds of discord to enable him or her to get the desired results, t which could be your loyalty or that of your counterpart or sometimes even both. Little incidents are blown out of proportions and tensions are escalated in the process. Eventually, the relationship is broken down beyond repair. You on one end are hurt by the accusations, and your peer is hurt by the counter accusations. Neither of you realizing that a third party took advantage of the emotional aspirations for each other (and yes, there is such a thing) and manipulated you into the current state you are in.

This goes on to say that our aspirations and ambitions are not always about the material things that we want. It is also reflected in our perceptions and expectations from the relationships in our lives. Dark psychology is employed by the predators among us to alter this perception and manipulate it to their own advantage.

Dark Psychology

EMOTIONAL SCARS

It has been said, "time heals all wounds".
I do not agree. The wounds remain.
In time, the mind, protecting its sanity covers them
with scar tissue and the pain lessens
But it is never gone.

Rose Fitzgerald Kennedy

One of the largest residual effects of every experience we have is emotions. They say that in life, experience is the best teacher. Having spent more than a decade trying to understand human nature, I am inclined to agree. Let me share one of my most memorable experiences from travels in recent times. I think it best illustrates the point I am trying to make. Every year, I pack up my bags and travel to explore places that are not really hot spots for tourists, but they are exotic all the same. On this particular trip, I was travelling with a tribe of natives on their annual pilgrimage journey to pay homage to a particular deity. I was not a worshipper, but they were kind enough to let me travel in their company and observe their routines. At night, as we sat by the campfire enjoying the warm glow in the dark after a nice meal, I listened to them chatter in a language I didn't understand.

My translator occasionally chimed in when there was a general laughter or question directed specifically at me. But for most part, I just observed. And that was when I saw this child, not more than 8 or 9 months, I think. I can't really tell at that age. Only that the child was crawling towards the fire. I looked around the fire, but no one seemed to be paying any attention. So, I made a move to intercept the child, but I was immediately reprimanded. All the interpreter told me was that the child was about to learn a valuable lesson, and I was concerned. The fire pit wasn't blazing hot, but some of the wood still had fire on them and there were embers lying about that was still glowing. I watched keenly.

The child, fascinated by the little flames, crawled closer and then stopped. Perhaps the heat from the fire had given him a pause. But then the brave lad decided to brave the heat and proceed. He paused at a safe distance and then held out his hand toward the flame which he promptly withdrew. His face registered a shocked expression, and I could see his lower lip quivering. I wanted to go to him but the man beside me must have sensed my intentions because he signaled me to wait. The poor baby's expression shifted from hurt to one of confusion. It was like he was telepathically speaking to the flame and asking why it hurt. He tried using his hand again, and this time he cried. The men cheered and laughed. A woman, quite possibly his mother, who must have been standing very close by quickly swooped in and carried him away.

I was incensed. I asked the translator the purpose of this. The chief responded through the translator with words that I still remember to this day. He said, it is hard to look at fire from a distance and argue against the eyes that such a glorious thing could also be deadly. Sometimes, one's hand must do the convincing when eyes fail. It is called experience. He went on to assure me that no one would have let anything dangerous happen to the child, but I get the feeling that his definition of dangerous is way different from what I imagine it to be. Now, before we veer off in righteous indignation (and rightly so) over cultural childcare practices, we should not neglect the stark truth in his words. There are lessons in life only experience can teach you, and each experience leaves an emotional scar.

There are certain experiences in life that would promptly induce the never again reaction from us. Those experiences are so deeply etched on our minds that we immediately interpret certain signs as a precursor to the event that scared us in the first place. And the second we observe these signs; our fight or flight instincts kick especially if those experiences pose a threat to us. This predictable pattern of behavior is meant to protect us in times of perceived danger. Think of it as a biological defense against what might cause us harm, or that emergency drill your body undergoes your brain senses you are in danger. What I have described here is the body's reaction to fear, but fear is not the only emotion that can be triggered by your experiences. There is a long spectrum of emotions, ranging from anger to zealousness, that can be triggered by an experience.

A woman in love memorizes her lover's scent. And every time she gets a whiff of that scent, her mood is transformed. Sometimes, it induces joy and on certain occasions, it can trigger lust. If that relationship packs up, the scents could induce sadness or rage depending on how bad the break up was. All I am saying is that emotions are part of the human experience. When we feel a certain way, we act a certain way. Certain events can trigger emotions that cause us to react abnormally. My near drowning experience as a teenager causes me to panic every time, I close my eyes under a shower. These reactions are triggered by the emotional scars we carry. Now, let me explain the science of this. When an event occurs, whether good or bad, your brain identifies that incident with a specific emotion. This would explain why something as simple as the smell of freshly baked bread can transport you to your childhood (if this was your experience).

Numerous marketing companies and advertising agencies employ this knowledge in their advertising strategy. They try to identify their product with things, experiences, or events they know appeal to you or other people like you (their target demography). Subconsciously, your brain correlates those activities or experiences with their products or services. To sell a barbecue grill, they don't come and say, "Hey, here is our awesome barbecue grill. Buy it." Instead, they feed you with images of a fun 4th of July family backyard cookout. You typically see kids running around happily, smiling grandparents chatting up some family member and the teenagers doing something cool. All of these interspersed with a nice beef cut simmering on the grill. It is almost as if they are saying if you buy this grill, you also buy into this experience. In other words, you were visually manipulated into making a purchase.

This is not necessarily sinister per se. But the regular people we meet in our everyday lives can prey on this weakness. If you are easily emotionally triggered, you can be manipulated into making rash decisions on anything from impulse purchase to falling for people on emotional principle alone. People can disguise themselves and make themselves into something they are not. They wear clothes and perfumes that make it seem as though they are wealthy and because you have a strong emotional connection with wealth, you look past other warning signs and make a regretful decision. Whether good or bad, your emotional scars can make you vulnerable to deception and manipulation.

PART FOUR:

RECOGNIZING AND IDENTIFYING YOUR REALITY

Dark Psychology

ACKNOWLEDGING THE LIES WE TELL OURSELVES

Above all, don't lie to yourself.

The man who lies to himself and listens to his own lie

comes to the point that he cannot distinguish the truth within him,

or around him and so loses all respect for himself and others.

And having no respect, he ceases to love.

Fyodor Dostoevsky

There are so many forms of lies we hear every day. Sometimes, the lies are told to protect you from something. It could be something as trivial as keeping the knowledge of something you are not ready to know; for example, a surprise birthday party. Sometimes, the lies are more complicated but not told entirely out of malice like the telling a person about their cheating spouse. The point is, for good for or bad, we all tell lies, but no lie is more grievous than the lies we tell ourselves. There is more danger from the lies we tell ourselves than the lies that other people tell us (this would be discussed extensively in the next chapter) and here is why.

In the previous chapter, I talked about the body's biological defense when the brain senses danger or situations that threaten us. These impulses, however irrational, may seem meant to protect us. Lying to yourself deadens those instincts and opens us to possible dangers. It is like seeing a speeding car coming down the highway and making up your mind to run across the road anyway. Instinctively, your body knows that this situation is precarious. A slight miscalculation could result in a fatal accident. But instead of waiting for the car to pass, you convince yourself that you are faster than the car or that the car is farther away than it looks, or it is not speeding as fast as it appears to be. These are the kind of lies we tell ourselves.

Self-deception occurs in many forms. But the most popular form of self-deception is denial. We convince ourselves that the threat is not real or imminent, so we make risky choices that we quickly come to regret. Denial is not always a clear-cut case of admitting that something does or does not exist. Sometimes, it is masked as optimism in the face of a very dire situation. And in some cases, the very opposite happens. You are in a good situation but choose to be pessimistic and deny the possibilities. According to a school of thought, humans are more susceptible to self-deception because we choose to hold on to certain beliefs. Say for instance, you meet this amazing person who seems to match all of your criteria in dealing with such a person. But underneath that layer, you can sense a withholding or even know outrightly that you are being deceived but rather than act on that instinct, you choose to act on the hope that people can be what they appear to be.

We hear of the expression wolf in sheep clothing all the time. There is no doubt that the wolf may be really good at disguising himself for the sheep just as there is no doubt that the sheep on some primal level were aware of the wolf in their midst but chose to deny the existence of the threat because they wanted to believe that the wolf was one of them. We can all imagine how that story played out. This pattern of behavior over time would dim the alarms bells that resound in our senses whenever a crisis arises because of what we tell ourselves.

Next to denial is rationalization. Denial and rationalization are tools of the same trade. They work handily together in self-deception. Rationalization is essentially how you explain away the situation. I have had female friends (and some of my male friends too in the same boat) who are in a relationship that isn't really healthy for them but rather than end things by taking themselves out of the equation, they somehow always seem to generate more reasons why they should stay put in that relationship. Women in abusive relationships know that a man raising his hand against you is displaying the highest form of disrespect. But I have heard these violent men been described as affectionate and their occasional violence being just one of their ways of showing the woman that they care. This behavior does not only apply to relationships.

People have found themselves working at a place they know exploiting them. But, they tell themselves how jobs are difficult to find and how they would not be able to pay the bills if they leave. And so, they continue to work under those terrible conditions refusing to even protest because they have come to accept the situation as normal thanks to their rationalizations and denials. Whether in our careers or in our normal relationships, a lot of us a leading sad and unfulfilled lives because we have convinced ourselves that we cannot do otherwise, and this is our fate. Some people even go a step further and say they deserve what they are getting because of some misdeed in the past. In other words, they have chosen to open the doors to their own prison cells, lock themselves in and then proceed to act as jailer. Self-deception is a mental prison of some sort but there are merits to it, too.

When confronted with challenges that threaten to overwhelm us, a little bit of self-deception can help to bolster your confidence and even the playing field. You may choose a more positive phrase other than self-deception to describe it, but it doesn't change what it is. People like to call it perp talk, getting psyched or giving yourself a morale boost…whatever you choose to call it, it still boils down to you convincing yourself about something that you are not. A man wanting to approach a very beautiful woman who he feels is out of his league has to convince himself that he is all that. He acts more confident than he actually feels in order to convince himself that he is indeed confident. So, you see, the self-confidence thing can swing both ways. But to avoid falling victim to people who use elements of dark psychology to get their way, you need to recognize the truth for what it is.

If your instincts are kicking in, rather than deny it, ask questions. Find out why you feel the way you do about the person and try to get more answers. When you learn to trust your instincts, you are better able to protect yourself. If a situation is not working out favorably for you, rather than choosing to be powerless about it (because yes, it is choice), you should actively look for a way to escape the situation. Don't lie to yourself. The truth may not be what we want it to be, but you should not have to live out a painful lie just to deny it. Recognize the lies you tell yourself for what they really are.

Dark Psychology

IGNORE THE LIES THAT OTHERS TELL US

> *Lies and secrets...*
>
> *they are like cancer in the soul*
>
> *They eat away what is good*
>
> *And leave only destruction behind.*
>
> **Cassandra Claire**

We are all victims of lies at some point in our lives. That doesn't mean everyone who came into our circle and lied to us was trying to use us to carry out some evil plan of theirs. In fact, there are truths that when told with malicious intent can have the same effect as a terrible lie if not worse. Whether the lies are coming from your best friend, a parent, or even someone from work, the effect can be devastating. In some cases, it is not the lie itself that hurts. It is the knowledge that someone you trusted made the deliberate choice to fabricate a story and convince you that it is real. Certain lies are told by simply not saying anything about it. People think, if I didn't say anything, I didn't lie about it. But in reality, that is called a lie by omission.

It is almost impossible to start with just one lie and leave it at that. One lie leads to another lie that perpetuates another lie until both the person telling the lie and the person being lied to are caught in a tangled web of lies. This web can be so tangled that extricating the truth becomes impossible. Lies have a way of changing you and that change is not always good. This is because you are being fed a fabricated version of reality. Against our better judgement, we buy into these lies and the anger we feel when the truth is unveiled is not entirely directed at the liar in question. We blame ourselves for believing those lies.

When we discover we are being lied to, we often react not just to the person and what they represent, our identity is also being called into question. Your loss of faith is not just in person but in yourself as well. The loss of faith results in doubts. And doubts lead to distrust. But before we get into the effect of lies, let us explore why we fall for the lies in the first place.

I am going to start off with the general populace and then proceed to bring things closer to home. If you have been active online, you will likely notice that the most read and followed stories are the sensational pieces. In recent times, there has been an increase in the pedaling of stories that have no truth to them. Even the prestigious Rolling Magazine which has always been known for their excellent reportorial skills had put up a story (which they believed to be true) that turned out to be false. So, you wonder, how come people with years of skills and experience were able to fall for that kind of lie? If you are expecting some kind of grand revelation of truth, I am sorry to disappoint you. The reason is quite simple and naturally a very human response. They wanted to believe it.

In the same way, we fall for the lies that people tell us because we want to believe that it is true. This happens on several levels and it is not always linked to people that are very close to us. For instance, if you share a certain political view or opinion, you are more likely to be following or reading articles or posts that support your belief. If someone tells a lie that supports your belief, you are more inclined to fall for that lie because you want it to confirm your own personal beliefs or theories. This also applies in our relationships as well. You believe that love should be a certain way and because a person displays patterns that correspond with what your idea of love is meant to be, you choose to ignore the other tell-tale signs and believe in their lies instead.

Another reason we believe a lie is because we have a personal stake in the lie. A manipulator presents you with an alternative reality that you suspect to be false but because your own personal interest conflicts with the truth, you chose instead to accept the lie. The personal interest may not just be about a personal gain. It could be your special feelings about the person. You like the person, and you have created this halo around that individual. So, you would rather stick to your haloed version of events (self-deception at work here) than face the possible reality that this person may be more sinister than he or she looks and that their ulterior motives may not be for your own best interests at all.

Lies that stem from an altered reality of events are not the only type of lies that can be used to manipulate us. When we think of people lying to us, we are more focused on events that were fabricated for the benefit of the liar, but there are other kinds of lies out there that can be as vicious, if not more, than the altered reality. I am referring to lies that are told to change your perception about yourself. Throughout every chapter in this book, I have strongly emphasized that we are most vulnerable when our emotions come to the forefront, especially when those emotions are spiraling out of control. When a manipulator meets a person who appears to be emotionally stable, he or she knows that it would be difficult to work their devious charms on such a person. So, one's first line of action is to wear down the emotional foundation of that person.

A manipulator looks for chinks in the person's proverbial armor and begin to exploit it. Let's say you are normally a confident person, but you have some insecurities about your body. A master manipulator would key into that concern and twist it by amplifying your fears. It may not come off as a direct insult, but it would be strategically used to imply that the problem is worse than it actually is. Snide remarks about how big you look today to how you need to cut back on the carbs are subtle but effective hints at the problem they are hoping to amplify. When you start accepting these lies, you would find yourself pondering on problems that really aren't issues in the first place. And gradually, the proverbial mole becomes the mountain, and you are promptly buried under insecurities that have eaten away at your confidence until you are exactly what the manipulator wants you to be: a person with poor self-esteem and zero confidence who can be easily manipulated.

If chirping away at your self-esteem does not get the desired results, a manipulator then tries the negative route. Telling you that you cannot do something and using your past experiences and emotions to support this lie until you believe it. Sometimes, the reverse is the case. You are lulled into a state where you feel secure even though the reality is different. This tactic is often used when the perpetrator wants to extract something like money or a favor from you.

Dark Psychology

He or she uses positive reinforcements rooted in lies to give you a false sense of security and then one strikes. It takes mental clarity and effort to see through the lies that people tell in whatever form they appear.

James W. Williams

DWELLING ON THE PAST

I have learned that if you must leave a place that you have lived in and loved and where all your yesteryears were buried deep, leave it any way except a slow way, leave it the fastest way you can.
Never turn back and never believe that an hour you remember
is a better hour because it is dead.
Past years seem safe ones, vanquished ones,
while the future lives in a cloud, formidable from a distance.

Beryl Markham

In a track race, athletes are trained to stay focused and ground themselves in the present. There is no looking back figuratively and literally. Their senses are attuned to the moment. When the race begins, it is all about them, the track, and the finish line. This is because, the second they start paying attention to anything else but the race, they start losing the race. Even in a relay race where the athlete has to look back and take the baton from their running mates, their gaze promptly returns to the track in front of them as soon as the baton exchanges hands. Life is like a race and looking back on the past can distract and hold you back from being the best you can be. And most importantly, this kind of distraction is the type of thing a manipulator would love to use against you.

Dark Psychology

When the brain is not actively triggering emotions that stems from memories, our mind does a bang-up job of bringing all those emotions to the forefront. I tried to think of how to best explain the firm grip our past can have over us and a scene from one of my favorite movies illustrates this. Without going into the plot of the movie [Pacific Rim], let me set the scene for you. Mako and Raleigh are paired up to try out the Jaeger [a machine designed to destroy the aliens] for the first time and to manipulate the machine, there has to be a mental connection through what they called the mental link. The connection process takes you through a series of memories [your past] before you are rooted in the present. Mako's recollection of her past is so vivid that she becomes trapped in it. This results in her detachment from the present reality. This detachment almost results in her activating a nuclear weapon that could have destroyed the present. Bringing it back to us, our reconnection with our past may not be as vivid, but the psychological threat that dwelling on the past poses is just as potent.

When we talked about emotional scars earlier, we explored the pains/emotions triggered by events and the focus was on our biological defense mechanisms. We know that the brain interprets certain signs from our environment as threats and in so doing, it activates reactions that we are not always able to control. This is somewhat similar to that except this time, we are actively engaging a negative experience by thinking consistently on it. And in that process, we unleash an avalanche of emotions that could put us under. Psychologists refer to this as ruminating. Just like a goat [or cow] regurgitates the food it ate hours prior and chews on it, we have a tendency to regurgitate our experiences and dwell on them.

But it is not just the negative past that we cling to sometimes, the past has a lot of positive memories that provide us with comfort. This connection makes it difficult to let go of it. Unfortunately, it is just as easy to become disillusioned with the positive past as it is with a negative past. We all know someone in our life who is fond of using the phrase, "the good old days," and we recognize how heartbreaking it can be to watch them cling to the remnants of the so-called glory days. You may not use that phrase, but your fondness of the past can get you quickly stuck in that memory and set you on a path that destroys your chances in the present. Of course, you may want to argue that if bad memories dredge up bad emotions, then good memories bring up good emotions and that cannot be bad. The truth is, as long as it is disconnecting you from the present reality, it is bad. And this is what dark psychology exploits.

When you live your life in the past, you get yourself rooted in a situation that either slows you down or stop you from moving forward. Fear is one of the most powerful emotions that our memories can activate. And it is not just the famous fear of the boogieman [or whatever inspires serious fear in you] that keeps you down. The fear of uncertainty can also hold you back. You might be holding on to a certain relationship, job or lifestyle simply because you are afraid of what would happen if that thing or person is no longer in your life. And that fear keeps you there even when the situation is not ideal for you.

This is not denial because you are aware of the wrongness of the situation. You have just decided to put your focus on what was and distance yourself or worse, accepted what is because you are afraid of what will/might be. Besides, you should believe that manipulators and saboteurs in your life would capitalize on this fear and work their deviousness to exploit this knowledge until they can get what they want. Their modus operandi would be to somehow strengthen the grip that this past has on you and convince you that the present reality is a necessity. They use your insistence on focusing on the past to discredit your present and rob you of a future. The irony here is that you are at least partially aware of what is happening, but you have made a conscious or subconscious decision remove yourself from the equation, so you justify your decision with an event that has already happened.

In essence, you yourself have created this illusion of the absence of choice and given the reins of your presence to others. This is not to say that looking back is completely wrong. Rear view mirrors were created specifically for this purpose. The point here is, if you really want to separate the truth from the lies, staying rooted in the present is one way to go about it. Psychologists say that people who dwell on the past are more likely to be depressed than others. Depression is one of those dark emotions that leave you vulnerable. And if you do get into treatment for the depression, one of the steps to overcoming it is to retrace your steps in the past, coming to terms with the reality of the situation, and then applying the lessons learned from the revisited past before letting go.

If you have a problem letting go, you only need to remind yourself that you have absolutely no control over what has happened. No matter how much you revisit it and dwell on it, you cannot change what has happened. The same can be said of the future. There are many possibilities. Sure, the steps you take now could to an extent determine what happens tomorrow but there are too many variables to accurately predict the future. What you own and have total control over is what you do right now. Detach yourself from the past and from the fears of the future and put your focus on the "right now."

Dark Psychology

BLIND OPTIMISM

I am not interested in blind optimism,
But I am very interested in optimism that is hard won.
That takes on darkness and then says, "that is not enough."

Colum McCann

When we accept responsibilities in life, we do so with gusto and enthusiasm. And as with everything in life, we encounter challenges which could range anywhere from mild obstacles to raging storms that seem to be bent on destruction...our destruction. In those times, your zeal and enthusiasm might wane. What keeps you from giving up and gets you through that rough patch is optimism. But there are different levels to this thing called optimism and not all of them have the same positive impact in our lives. There is a kind of optimism that appears to disconnect you from the reality and that type of optimism is known blind optimism. But before we get into that, let us look at that aspect of human nature that makes us want to believe in an alternate outcome even when we are facing a very dire situation. Just like the author of the quote above, we are interested in what makes us unflinching in the face of darkness.

Like all facets of human emotional behavior, it appears that we are simply hardwired to be optimistic, not just in the face of danger. This behavior is present in our simple everyday activities. You have a product that is maybe a few days past its expiry date, but you go ahead to eat it anyway in the hope that it would not cause any harm to you. Or you are approaching the traffic lights just as it changes colors and rather than slow to a stop, so you speed up in the hope that you would make it past the lights without getting caught. Or maybe you are even taking the chance to ask a person out in the hopes that he or she would feel the same way about you, as opposed to throttling over your exposed feelings on the floor with a sledgehammer? It is part of your emotional reflex. Despite Murphy's Law, you are optimistic because you are human.

However, some people take this optimistic approach in their dealings a tad too far. Instead of just pushing the boundaries as I illustrated with the examples above, they put absolute faith in the possibility that the good outcome they are hoping for would outweigh the likelihood of things going wrong. This kind of thinking inspires a reckless behavior that could have a painful ending if the emotion is not checkmated. Being optimistic delivers many health and mental benefits. If you have ever read the book, *The Power of Positive Thinking* by Norman Vincent, you are no doubt furnished with information on just how well positive thinking can serve you. Medical studies show that people who are optimistic are more than likely to recover from life-threatening sicknesses than people who are the opposite. Overall, optimism can blind you.

Blind optimism is a form of self-deception. In this case, you are not just thinking that you have a good chance of getting the desired positive outcome. You have deluded yourself into thinking that things would play out the way you hoped they would: because they are banking on the positives of the situation, they do not take any steps to protect themselves in the event that things go awry because they are not even entertaining any negative notion. When you are blinded by optimism, you have a higher tendency to rationalize and explain away the reality of the situation. Even when you are presented with the gravity of the situation, your blind optimism keeps you from taking any action that would mitigate negative outcomes.

As I said earlier, we fall for a lie because we want to do so. Blind optimism is a kind of lie that also works in distancing us from the reality of things. You find yourself confronting a lie directly in the face, but perhaps because accepting the reality that this person or situation is not what they seem or appear to be might be too hurtful, we turn on the optimism switch a notch higher. Our need to want to believe that people are not as terrible as they may be makes us give in to demands that have a negative impact on us. In turn, we replace that negative gut instinct with a bright reaction straight out of the pages of the book of blind optimism. And often times, we do this because we want to feel good about the situation or about the person.

Blind optimism affects your ability to accurately assess the pitfalls and problem areas in any given situation. It puts you in a mental state where you are almost walking on clouds and gives you a false sense of security. You feel invincible to the risks and fail to take precautions. The plus side of blind optimism is that you are more likely to take on risks than most. In business, people who are blindly optimistic are usually in the early adopters' category. When a new product hits the market, while others are busy calculating the risks and trying to assess their odds, these guys dive in feet first. Many new business counts on these types of people.

In day to day living, blind optimism creates a dangerous detachment from reality. It is like a person who wakes up in the morning and decides that he wants to skydive. Giving no thought to altitudes, weather conditions or landscape, he just buckles on his parachute and dives. The chances of hitting a rock before deploying one's parachute is just as high as making it to the ground in one piece. But one chooses to prepare for only the reality that one is willing to accept. You cannot deal with people in the same manner and not expect some sort of negative backlash. There is ignorance and then there is the willingness to see the danger ahead and chose to do nothing about it. It doesn't matter if this person is your best friend, your mother, or your partner. If you spot the signs that could imply something else is at work, wishing and hoping that you are wrong is not going to protect you if you are right. Sure, it might temporarily keep that relationship in a good place, but in the long run, even that too would disintegrate. Taking off the blindfold would require you being truthful with yourself.

There is a common saying that the truth is bitter. I wish I could say that this wasn't the case. When it comes to your relationships with people, bitter is an understatement in the description of the truth. Confronting the reality of the situation can birth a pain that you never imagined and for a while, it is going to hurt. In a situation where your emotions are being taken advantage of, you cannot afford to bury your head in the sand because you don't want to face the reality of your experience. Even a gradual revelation is not helpful. What you need to do is rip off the Band-Aid and face the emotions squarely. The truth hurts, but it will also set you free. You just need to remind yourself that it is all that this

Dark Psychology

pain is all part of the process and the hurting brings you one step closer to healing.

James W. Williams

THE VICIOUS CYCLE

*Once you believe that things are permanent,
you are trapped in a world without doors.*
Genesis P. Orridge

The four walls that imprison us in a web of deceit are the lies we tell ourselves, the lies that others tell us, dwelling on the past and blind optimism. Each of them is a facet of the false realities that entraps us and on their own, they can have a ghastly impact on us, but when you have all the elements working together, the results can be devastating. People who have escaped or lived through lives where they were manipulated incessantly can identify at least 3 of these elements at work when the manipulations were at its peak.

As with all forms of deceptions, it starts out with a lie. The lie is not easily discernable in the beginning. Perhaps, on an instinctive level, you get the sense that something is not right, but there is almost nothing concrete to base your feelings on, so you decide to go with the lie. The decision to go with the lie does not always happen on its own. You don't just accept the lie. On a personal level, you would have to convince yourself to believe the lie and this usually requires you lying to yourself. You remind yourself it is not as bad as it looks. You tell yourself that this person has no reason to lie to you. Basically, you convince yourself anything you need to convince yourself that your instincts are wrong. To help give substance to the lie you are reiterating, you throw in a good measure of unrealistic expectations under the guise of being optimistic. This optimism further impairs your better judgement and leaves you even more vulnerable than you initially were. And to eliminate any doubts, you draw on a past experience to validate your present choices and from there things go downhill. The situation does not always play out like this. Sometimes, one come comes before the other, but the objective is the same: to trap and deceive you.

When this cycle is in play, the manipulator becomes the puppeteer and you become the puppet. The strings with which they use to pull you around would be your emotions. They jerk you around to do their biddings. Now it is important to remember that a person's ability to successfully manipulate another does not make them a diabolical master planner. These events often play out to a natural order of things. When you leave something of value outside your home and a thief comes along and swipes it, you cannot say that he or she plotted the incident. By nature, these people have groomed themselves to be takers. Whether they have the consent of the owner or not, they are inclined to just take especially when it is put out there for them. In the same vein, a manipulator is inclined to turn the emotions of others against him or her to work to one's own personal advantage. Emotions are to a manipulator what a wand is to a magician, and con artists use emotions to their advantage.

There is a broad spectrum of emotions that the average human experiences. And knowing that emotions are the tools that manipulators use to exploit us might make you want to instinctively shut down your emotions. And I can relate with that line of thinking. But the truth is, numbing your emotions could have an adverse negative effect. For starters, numbing your emotions could lead to you trying to find escape in other places like drugs and alcohols, which gives you the illusion of being not feeling when in actuality, it amplifies your feelings. Besides, the choice to numb your emotions [if such a thing was possible] would mean not experiencing the good stuff as well. Because, while you want to purge negative emotions like greed, anger and sadness, you want to experience joy, happiness and peace, too. The emotions are some of the things that make sour existence as human that more valuable and getting rid of these emotions would be akin to living in a world without color. Instead of trying to numb these emotions, we can exert more control over them and use them to help us grow as individuals.

And this brings us to the next important topic. Control. While manipulators work with our emotions against us, their biggest weapon is having us believing that we have no control. This grand illusion has us thinking we are powerless and helpless and there is nothing we can do about it. But if you review this section of the book, heck if you go all the way back to the beginning, you will realize something very interesting. The common denominator in all of this is you and for their plans to work, it requires some form of consent from your part. I am not saying that what has happened or is happening to you is your fault. No, far from it. All I am trying to say is that you are not as helpless as you seem. One of the reasons I wrote the book is to help those who are under the influences of dark psychology to escape and overcome its hold. And the first step to achieving this is embracing the powers you have. Your emotions can make you vulnerable, but with the right application of knowledge, your emotions can equally become your greatest ally in this battle.

Dark Psychology

You have a choice and you have a voice. Don't let anyone convince you otherwise. In the next chapter, we will examine in depth how to break free from the whole. Right now, I want you to look inward as though you are looking into the mirror. Embrace your emotions: the fear, the rage, the pain. These feelings are all a part of you. It may not paint a perfect picture, but for one moment, put your expectations for perfection on the shelf. Focus instead on what you feel right now. Whether those emotions are good or bad, make a choice to want better for yourself. The sky would not open, there will be no celestial music playing somewhere in the heavens and your situation will not change overnight. On the contrary, things might have to get worse before they get any better. But when you make this choice, you are mentally preparing yourself for what is to come next.

And if you need a more tangible reason to push for this sudden upheaval from what you have come to accept as your comfort zone, remind yourself that you are enough reason for this to happen. You deserve better, your opinions matter and there is no other person who is more powerful and more instrumental in influencing this change that you desire than you. Right up to this moment, you have looked out for others. You tailored your needs to suit the expectations of others, you put aside your sense of self in other to accommodate the needs of others and for long, you have stayed on the back shelf and depreciated in value. But no more. Now is the time to look out for your own interest and there is no shame in that. That negative voice or the manipulator in your life would want to tell that you are being selfish. Counteract this obvious lie with the truth. The truth is that your ability to care and look out for others begins with the choice to look after yourself first. Therefore, you are being "selfish" at the moment is the best step you can take to becoming selfless.

PART FIVE:

HOW TO BREAK FREE

James W. Williams

ACCEPT THAT YOU HAVE A PROBLEM

Often times, it's not about becoming a new person, but becoming the person you were meant to be, and already are but don't know how to be.
Heath L. Buckmaster

We often dwell more on the opinion of others and prioritize how the world sees us or how we want the world to see us. The lifestyle trend of this current age has its own slogan, "fake it until you make it." This kind of approach to living causes us to have a fast and loose relationship with reality. We are so caught up in faking it that we are unable to pull off the mask even when we are alone with ourselves. This form of self-deception can ingrain itself so deeply in our lives that we might wake up one day and find ourselves in a situation that greatly contradicts the fake reality we have worked so hard to preserve and sometimes shocks us to our very core. If we are to be entirely honest, we are not always caught off guard by the lies that are told to us. On some level, we know. What makes us off guard is how much we are hurt by it. And it is this hurt that makes us shy away from the problem in the first place. To break free, the first step is confronting the situation and breaking off any illusions. You cannot go any further if you do not shatter the illusions that surround you. Arm yourself with the knowledge that you have a choice. Then make the conscious choice to see things for what it is.

That deal that seems too good to be true might actually be just that...too good to be true.

Next, trust your gut instincts. There are times that a lie has been so masterfully fabricated that it appears to be true. But on some instinctive level, you can sense an imbalance between what should be, what is and then what is being projected to you. There may not be any physical signs to show that hey, something is wrong, but you have a sense that something is amiss. In times like that, it is easy to just dismiss those feelings and go with what you are being told. You may not want to appear rude or be perceived in a certain light, so you give in and ignore that inner voice. Learning to trust your instinct requires practice over time. You start by training yourself on small and simple things. Perhaps you are about to leave the house and you get the urge to go back in and check on something. Or maybe, you just thought of someone and felt the need to call him or her. These are tiny instances and may not lead to large payoffs, but it builds your confidence in your instincts, so that when situations of true consequence arise, you are better able to discern what your instincts are telling and act on them. If you are already in a situation and don't have the time to train your ability to trust your instincts, you should not lose hope. Your instincts are there to protect your best interests. And as long as you are alive, you have instincts that want to help you stay alive. In this situation, you just want to get out of it. So, what are your instincts telling you?

That question would lead you to this next step. Ask the right questions. Start with yourself. Try to find out why you feel the way you do. Look at your current situation and find out why you are no longer content with the way you feel. Ask yourself why you feel the way you do and see if you can be more specific about your feelings. I reiterated that emotions make you vulnerable, but they can also act as a guide when you feel lost. When you are not able to satisfactorily provide the answers you seek, look outside yourself. Looking outside yourself does not necessarily mean you should confront the predator although it may eventually get to this. I don't recommend going the direct route immediately as you will give the perpetrator an opportunity to present a defense that may further cloud your judgement and not get you the results you desire. It can also clue the person that you might be on to them. This might activate their own fight or flight response. Instead, look to people within your cycle of trust. Given that you are currently trying to navigate through a situation that involves a breach of trust, it may be difficult to suddenly decide who to trust. If you are really concerned about that, then go to someone who has little or no personal stake in the equation. Someone who is not directly related to you or the person(s) involved might be best. These people are more likely to be honest with you.

When you ask the questions, the next important thing is to listen to the answers. This may sound somewhat incredulous because duh, you are going to be listening to the answers. The reality is that our self-deception can cause us to be selective about the responses we get. We tell ourselves we are listening, but we are only really paying attention to the answers we want to hear instead of the answers we are actually getting. You may have shattered the illusions around you, but there is still a part of you that clings to the comfort that those illusions bring. The pain of confronting the reality of the situation would deter you from hearing the real answers to the questions you have asked. Actual listening requires some sense of detachment, but not from reality this time around. You need to detach yourself from your emotions.

Your detachment from our emotions could lead you to the next step which is processing the new information logically. Acting irrationally can complicate situations more than they already are. Letting all the emotions simmer and spring up to the surface makes your exit strategy that much difficult. The irrational part of you when confronted with the truth may want you to just let everything go to hell. Your anger, which is righteously justified, can spur you into taking steps that help pacify your emotions in the short term. But in the long term, you may come to regret those actions. I am not saying you should deny your emotions; I am suggesting don't act based on those emotions. Deal with the situations first and then your emotions later.

ACT QUICKLY

It's the action, not the fruit of the action that is important.
You have to do the right thing.
It may not be in your power,
may not be in your time that there will be any fruit.
But that doesn't mean you stop doing the right thing.
You may never know what results come from your action.
But if you do nothing, there will be no result.
Mahatma Gandhi

You have confronted the reality of your situation, which is usually the hardest part. However, it doesn't end there. You cannot hope that the situation would just go away on its own. Remember, you have a choice in this. Even your inaction is a deliberate choice you have made and like the great Mahatma Gandhi said, if you do nothing, there will be no results. Breaking free from a web of deceit might be exhilarating at first until you have to deal with the outpouring of emotions in the aftermath. The intensity of the emotions experienced may cause us to want to go into denial. And this is a normal process. In the five stages of grief, the first stage is denial. The more you delay in taking action, the deeper and faster your denial sets in. And when denial sets in, there is a very high probability that you would go back to the vicious cycle that characterized this stage of your life. Avoid this by taking prompt action now. It doesn't have to be anything grand.

Something as simple as informing your close friend of the reality of the situation can set in motion a series of events that will eventually set you free.

After making the choice to act, you should know that the fabric of illusion is made of tougher material than glass. While I used the term "shatter your illusion," what actually happens is a gradual separation of facts from fiction. With your emotions in high gear, the illusion might be working its way back into your heart by using fragments of your emotions to mend it. When a liar is caught in a lie, he or she may seek to recruit others to enforce that lie when the liar no longer has a hold over you. A deceptive partner, whom you have recently broken up with, might use the other mutual relationships in your life at this point to influence you into changing your mind. The person used may not even be in the liar's league, but he or she was probably just manipulated. Liars have no problems using friends, family and even a religious leader to get what they want. You have to stand up for the choice you have made and make up your mind to see it through.

When the ploy to manipulate you through other people fails, liars often resort to their old method, which is leeching onto your emotions. In divorce situations, spouses use their partner's emotional concerns for their child to drag them down. Threats like if you leave, you are never going to see the kids again are used. In business dealings, there is usually an implied threat to cut the other person off without any form of payment. This is a last-ditch effort by the manipulator to attempt to control their victim. They know that their cars are no longer effective and feeling threatened by their loss of control, they use power plays like this to attempt to gain the upper hand. Power plays usually involves forms of blackmail ranging from petty stuff to deep secrets that were entrusted to them when the relationship was good. The blackmailer may want to get financial payouts, more leverage in the negotiation deal, and for the more sinister individuals, one just seeks control.

At this point, one's actions may have you in a corner, making you want to lash out and react. I strongly advise against this. You will need both your logic and your instincts if you want to get out of this unscathed. Although, the truth of the situation is that when you discover you have been consistently lied to, you become emotionally scarred so, the question of leaving the situation unscathed becomes mute. However, priority should be given to taking the route that allows you to leave that toxic situation, without further harming yourself. Emotionally, you are all over the place. Rage, anger, hurt and disappointment are just a tip of the iceberg. But you need to think logically. Keep your head above water and be alert.

They say that an animal is more dangerous when it feels cornered. For a human, this sense of imminent fear is worse. When a person has been caught in the web of deceit woven by oneself, he or she tries to do everything to protect himself or herself. At that point in time, one's selfish instincts and protective mechanisms kick into overdrive, so one is willing to do anything to avoid facing the consequences of his or her actions. As with human nature, it is not possible to predict the extent they are willing to go to avoid this. So, rather than wave your agenda to bring them to justice in their face, your priority should be ensuring that you are safe. If it is possible, I would recommend a physical separation, even if it is temporary from the person who you feel is manipulating you. Not only does this help in giving you room to think clearly, it can help weaken the hold that they have over you. Being in the same proximity, especially if they are on their own territory can make you more vulnerable to more manipulations.

A Many liars and manipulators switch on their charms when they have been caught. They would appear deeply remorseful, apologetic and may even go to extreme lengths to try and convince you of their remorse. But don't fall for it as this could be just another act and another ploy to manipulate you into taking less drastic measures that they may not find favorable. If you feel your resolve weakening, get out at the very least. That action alone can make a huge difference.

GET HELP FAST

The best way to not feel hopeless is to get up and do something.

Don't wait for good things to happen to you.

If you go out and make some good things happen, you will fill the world with hope, you will fill yourself with hope.

Barrack Obama

When you find yourself trapped by the manipulations of others, one of the emotions you tend to experience is confusion. This contributes to clouding your rational thinking leaving with a sense of helplessness. At this point, you may even be questioning the reality of what you are facing. If you continue to entertain these doubts, it would lead to denial. You will probably want to conclude that you have gotten the entire situation wrong. Perhaps you misinterpreted certain things and came to the wrong conclusion? This kind of thinking will drive right back to the arms of the manipulator. Resist the urge to give in by getting a second opinion. In a health crisis, people go to another doctor to get a second opinion. This is to eliminate any iota of doubt you may have about the first diagnosis and affirm the best course of treatment for you. In the same way, getting the opinion of another person can help you discern the truth of the situation and what your next steps might be. Just remember, it is better to go to someone who has proven countless times that he or she has your best interest.

Now that you have the confirmation you need, do not try to take on the challenge on your own. The situation may not be something you want anyone else to know about. You may be worried that people would call you gullible for being where you are. The truth is that they probably will. But they are entitled to their own opinions. Don't let the fear of what people might say ruin your chance of creating a better life for yourself. You don't have to prove anything to anyone but yourself. The world can think what they want to think. Right now, your priority is coming out of the situation and surviving it enough to thrive. A lie may be small and petty, but when it is being told to with the goal of doing something that you didn't want to do, it hurts. It makes you question everything about yourself and stirs up this internal battle. You should not fan the flames of this battle by throwing in the opinions of people who have no idea what it would mean to walk in your shoes. If you need the extra bit of help, reach out for it and be willing to accept it. If you can handle the situation yourself, by all means please do. Just be certain that whatever decision you take, the goal is to get you out and not into the good books of other people. You deserve more than that.

When you have the help you need, the next step is to confront the perpetrator. I suggest you pick the scene or location for this. Chose somewhere that you know gives you the upper hand. This would require some careful planning on your part. If the perpetrator exists in the cyber world, you would have to involve the police and relevant authorities, especially if the person swindled you of your money. Do some preliminary investigation of your own. There are software applications that run facial recognition on popular social media sites like Instagram and Facebook. Look for clues to the person's true identity in the conversations you have had and only when you are armed with enough evidence, you should confront him or her. If the confrontation happens before you have evidence, you risk spooking them and sending him or her into one's hideouts. Of course, with the authorities involved, you would still get them eventually, but it could take longer than it normally would if you had patiently prepared yourself before doing the confrontation.

When it is someone who lives in close proximity to you, things may have to be done differently. If you fear for our life in any way, please do not confront this person on your own. In abusive relationships, it is best to avoid confrontations entirely. Simply bid your time and look for the best opportunity to escape. Don't succumb to demands about having "one last conversation". And if you must consent to a meeting like this, please ensure that you are not alone. Notify the people who care about you and have at least one person present during this meeting. Your safety is the priority. If you are in an abusive situation, I strongly advise these precautions:

Reach out to a local organization that caters to victims of abuse in your area. This is probably the best and most important step would take as they have professionals who are there to guide you and counsel you on your next course of action.

Dark Psychology

Get out while you can. Don't wait for that big pay, the right moment or some significant event. When you get the opportunity, take it and use it. Deal with the aftermath later. And if the opportunity does not present itself, have a safety plan that would lead to your escape. Do all you can to stay alive and as soon as the moment presents itself cease it.

After confronting the perpetrator and taking the necessary steps to leave the situation, you need to commence the healing process promptly. It doesn't matter the scale and gravity to which you were hurt, manipulated, or abused. You need to be able to move past it and waiting for time to "heal" your wounds requires more than sitting on your couch and reliving the past. Time will give you enough distance from your experience, but if you have acquired anything from this book, it is the fact emotional scars almost never heal. If you do not do something about it, an unhealthy scab could form over the wound leaving you just as vulnerable if not more than when you were living the experience. Talk to a counsellor, go to therapy, whatever you chose to do, take an active role in facilitating the healing process. It will not happen overnight, but each day and each step you take in therapy, the closer you will be to getting better.

DON'T COVER UP

It isn't the original scandal that gets people in the most trouble

...it is the attempted cover-up.

Tom Petri

To endure something as trying and traumatic as living with the lies of someone you trust, this trauma can produce a deep psychological effect. When I started this book, my goal was to help people sieve through the lies in their everyday environment and live above the manipulations of others. The entire focus of this book has been 80% on looking inward and the rest on helping you understand what dark psychology really is. But there is one aspect that we did not go into and this is something you are going to have to experience on your own. That aspect is the people who perpetrate these acts. I provided basic information to help you decode elements and traits of dark psychology but that is as far as I can go.

This is because, the people who are most likely to use you and manipulate you are people you have come to love and trust. The duration of the relationship you may have had with them does not guarantee that they are incapable of hurting you. Sometimes, the times spent with you helps cement your trust in them making you more vulnerable and more susceptible to their charms. That is not to say all the relationships you have would lead to some form of manipulation down the line or that strangers suddenly pose a lesser trait. My point is, there is no way to simply determine that this person is going to hurt you. The best you can do is look out for the signs I mentioned and keep an open mind because, you may struggle more with the idea that this person you trusted hurt you this way than the actual thing that was done to you.

In such a situation, your first impulse would be to deny. This denial hurts you more than it helps. Rather than cover up, you should face the embarrassing truth head-on. Recognize the situation for what it is. And try not to let your emotions cloud your ability to make rational decisions. Because yes, being manipulated sucks and people who do it deserve some form of punishment, but we all know that things are usually more complicated than that. What if the person is your sister, brother, spouse, best friend, spiritual leader? How then do you deal with it?

I would start by saying one's status in your life does not automatically make him or her immune to the consequences of one's actions. But there are other factors that might be adversely affected by whatever decision you take. So, the first thing you need to do is face the embarrassing truth that this person failed and hurt you with scheming and actions. Next, decide on if this relationship is worth continuing. Your partner cheating on you and lying about it all this while is terrible, but do you really what it to be the end of that relationship? Are there kids involved? What happens if you suddenly cut your partner off? You need to know that in a situation like this, cutting the person off is not the only answer. So, ask yourself the right questions. I would start off by asking, barring the offence they committed, how was the relationship? Was it good? Is it worth salvaging? Is the person ready to put in the amount of work required to make things right again? Are you ready to put in the work?

If you decided to call it quits, you would need to figure out how to manage the relationships that are linked to the fallout from this. If there are no ties, proceed to the next chapter on forgiving yourself. If there are ties, depending on the nature of the ties, both of you may have to come together with a narrative on how you want to proceed. If those ties are fickle, you can simply choose to go your separate ways without giving anyone any additional information as you owe them no explanation. Do your best to heal and move on without damaging any other relationship unless you have to. If you decide to continue with your relationship with the person, you have your work cut out for you because, it is going to be a hard, long uphill battle. You will get through it no doubt, but not without will and effort.

Both parties would have to show their willingness to heal the relationship. Apologizing profusely is a good start, they would need to do more than that. The fabric of trust has been ripped apart and mending it is going to require time effort and commitment to it. Both of you should be realistic in your expectations of each other. The person who defaulted will have to work hard on regaining your trust. And the person hurt will have to work hard at learning to believe that person again. There will be glitches in this initially, but the renewed commitment to keep at it daily will propel the relationship forward.

For starters, you might want to give each other space after the initial crisis. The space could be anything from a few days to a couple of weeks, but it should not exceed a month. Use this time to process your feelings about the incident. Try to separate the person from their action because as hurtful as their actions were, there are many factors that could have contributed to it. It may seem like making excuses, but it isn't. Circumstances can cause people to take certain actions, but those actions do not entirely define their character. If you have made the decision to mend this relationship, you may have to take this approach in your thinking.

Next, keep the line of communication open. I am not saying that you have to analyze every single thought between the two of you. Just don't shut each other out. Conversations may seem stifled at first, but with time, you guys can back into rhythm. Be honest in your conversations but try not to speak out of spite. Avoid bringing up the past every time you have an argument. Clinging to what has happened makes it difficult to go past it and grow to where you want to be. Stay rooted in the present. Remember, living in the past has no real benefit.

Above all, trust that you have made the right decision. When you discover that you have been manipulated and lied to, it is not just trust in others that is broken. It is trust in yourself as well. You question your judgement at every turn. Stay rooted in the present and trust that you have made the right and rational decision to mend things. But don't heighten the pressure on yourself by making it mandatory that the new relationship must work. Put in the effort, put in the time. But don't feel disappointed if things don't work out the way you were expecting.

FORGIVE YOURSELF

Take a walk through the garden of forgiveness
and pick a flower of forgiveness for everything you have ever done.
When you get to that time that is now,
make a full and total forgiveness of your entire life
and smile at the bouquet in your hands because it truly is beautiful.

Stephen Richards

People assume that when you have been wronged, the main party that requires forgiveness is the person that committed the offense in the first place. Usually, they are right. But in a situation like this one, where a relationship was established with the offender and that offender took advantage of the relationship, one of the unlikely people who require forgiveness is the victim. There is a reason why even when ties have been severed with the offender, you still find yourself experiencing emotions like depression, anger, irritability, anxiety, and mood swings among other things. These are normal emotions to experience, but you may not be experiencing them for the reasons you think. There is a very strong possibility that the reason for all of these emotions is guilt and shame. This guilt does not stem from something you think you did wrong. It is rooted in the thinking that you did something you were not supposed to do.

You feel guilty for being gullible, vulnerable and for generally putting yourself in a situation where you were easily manipulated in the first place. You are feeling guilty about the hurt you think you brought on yourself. We have all been in this situation at some point. We feel guilty that either our actions or inactions led to the hurt of others even though we were not directly involved in the perpetration of the act. The first thing you need to do is remind yourself that regardless of what happened, it is not your fault. You may not be able to change this perception overnight, but over time by constantly reminding yourself of this fact, you will start believing yourself. To further affirm this belief, you should also remind yourself that the lessons you have obtained from this has put you in a better position to protect yourself against any similar incident from occurring in the future.

The next thing is to accept that the past is not something you can change. It has happened, you have learned, and you have moved on. There is no need to keep reliving the experiences you had. Dwelling on the what ifs, what might have been, what you could have, should have and would have done cannot in any way change a single second of what has already happened. The best you can do is pick up the lessons you have learned and shape them into the new principles to live by. You have bravely accepted the reality of the situation despite the lies you were told. Now is the time to accept that this business was concluded in the past and it stays there. You may be dealing with the aftermath of the crisis, but that doesn't mean that it is still happening. Take each day as it comes and finds more reasons to look forward instead of looking backward. If you are feeling so anxious about the past, you can take out a day to re-enact the past. One way to do this is by having a mental re-do. Write down what you think you could have done to change things giving all that you do know now. And then move on from it. The purpose of this exercise is to give you some sort of control over what has happened. Take back your power and move on to the next thing.

Now that you have re-written the past, it is time for you to turn over the next page and begin the next chapter of your life. Start by tackling your regrets. These have a way of compounding our feelings. Accept that you did the best you could do under the circumstances and give yourself room to grow. Remember, yours was not a crime. You just had the misfortune of trusting the wrong person. Assign the blame to the right person. Using affirmatives like "I always fall for the wrong person" or "I am so gullible" is very self-limiting. Dig deeper into yourself to find out exactly where those thoughts are coming from. It is only when you have identified the underlying emotion that you can move past these negative affirmations. And the longer you accede to these negative phrases, the more acute your anxiety levels are going to get. This is because you might become somewhat paranoid about your relationships with people, seeing enemies only were friends and reading the wrong meaning in every action.

Finally, there is the issue of love. We may be harsh in our dealings with others but the person we are most harsh with is ourselves. We find it easier to forgive the perpetrator than to forgive ourselves and the cost of this behavior is self-destructive patterns that are evident in our other relationships. We sabotage those relationships before they even begin. Using the guise of preventing another manipulative relationship, we destroy new relationships. The real reason for this behavior is the loss of the feeling of self-love. Deep down inside, you don't feel you deserve love but because you would rather hear that from yourself, you burn bridges. There are pills to help you cope with the anxiety and depression, but there are no pills to get to that place where you fall completely in love with yourself. That would require some work and at the end of the day it is worth it. There are no hard or fast rules on how to begin this journey to self-discovery. However, I believe that waking yourself up daily with positive affirmations like, "I love myself and I deserve to be loved" is a start. It's cheesy at first, but highly effective in the long run.

And when you have resolved your issues with the past, forgiven yourself and begun the process of learning to love yourself, it is now time to let go. All that pain, all that negativity, all that anger…own it for a moment and then let go. All the steps listed in this chapter are great, but the healing process is only completed when you let go.

TRUST YOUR INSTINCTS

Trust your hunches.

They are usually based on facts filed away just below the conscious level.

Dr. Joyce Brothers

In one of the earlier chapters, we touched on this briefly. I decided to dedicate a whole chapter to this because when you are dealing with the forces of dark psychology, your primary defense against it is your instinct. While your brain is interpreting signals based on facts, logic and sometimes experience, your heart is working on the opposite end, sieving information through a filter of emotions. Your gut instinct is the only thing picking up vibrations that neither the heart nor the brain can explicate. And if you can groom yourself to that point where you recognize your inner voice and are trained to react to it, you reduce your chances of being seduced by people trying to work their manipulative will on you.

For starters, recognizing this voice is hard. And that is because over the course of our lives, we have allowed voices of doubt, self-discrimination as well as the loud voices of the critics within and without to drown out our authentic voice. This voice or instinct is hinged on your survival. So, trust that when it kicks in, it senses things in your immediate vicinity that your brain neurons can yet process. Some people call it intuition, and some refer to it as instinct, they are undoubtedly the same thing especially when it comes to relationships. To begin trusting your instincts, you have to accept that it may not always make logical sense. If you have ever been in the middle of doing something and suddenly experienced the sensation of being watched, then you know what I am suggesting. You have no eyes at the back of your head, there is no one else in the room with you but you get the tiny shiver that runs down your spine and a "sudden knowledge" that you are being watched. That is exactly what I am talking about.

The first step to connecting with your instinct is decluttering your mind of the voices that you have let in. You can do this with meditation. Forget the "he said, she said" chatter. Focus on your center. That voice that you know is you. Next, pay attention to your thoughts. Don't just dismiss those eclectic monologues you have in your head. Instead go with the flow of the thoughts. Why do you think a certain way about a certain person? How come you feel so deeply about this person even though you have only known each other for a couple of days? What is this nagging feeling you have about this other person? As you explore your thoughts, you become more attuned with your intuition and understand when your instincts kick and how to react to it. If you are the kind of person who prefers to make spur of the moment decisions, you may need to learn to take a step back to pause and think. This moment where you pause gives you a chance to really reflect on and evaluate your decisions.

The next part is a hard part and not many people would be able to follow through on it. Unfortunately, this is not a step you can skip or navigate around. This part involves trust. To be able to trust your instinct, you have to be open to the idea of trusting yourself and trusting others. Your inability to trust others would just make you paranoid and when you are paranoid, it is not your instincts that kick. It is your fear. Fear has the tendency of turning every molehill into a mountain. You have to let go of your fear, embrace trust and let that lead in your new relationships. Without the roadblocks put up by fear in your mind, you are better able to hear the voice within.

Finally, you need to re-evaluate your priorities. If money and material possessions are at the forefront of your mind, you may not be able to see past them. Every interaction you have with people would be interpreted as people trying to take advantage of you and if you dwell on this often enough, it soon becomes your reality. You know how you attract what you think of into your life. If you are constantly thinking about material wealth, you will only attract people who think the same way as you.

Using this as a guide, view all of your relationships; the old, the new and the perspective with this new hindsight. Don't go into a relationship expecting to be played. Whether it is a business relationship, a romantic relationship or even the regular acquaintance, be open when you approach them. That way, you can get the right feedback from your intuition about them. Also, don't step into this thinking that your gut is going to tell you to run in the opposite direction when you meet people who are suspect. It would be a small simple nudge.

I remember an experience I had during one of my travels. I got into this cab. There was nothing physically that I can point out to say this triggered me. I just know that I had this sudden revulsion for the driver. I was overwhelmed by this smell of sweaty armpits. I am not very big on body odors, but I have been caught in situations where I just had to grin and bear it [elevator rides anyone?]. But in this case, I just wanted to get out of his cab. As soon as we pulled into a prominent well-lit spot, I asked to exit, even though it wasn't my stop. Just as I came down, a squad car pulls up next to him. Apparently, the authorities had been notified of its involvement in the robbery and kidnap case. I don't know if he had the same plans for me. All I knew was that the moment I entered; I could not get out fast enough. My instinct did not tell me to run or that hey, your driver is a kidnapper. It just made me feel like there was something wrong about being in the car. It was that simple.

In the same way, your instincts speak to you using a language you understand. Whether it is chills down your spine, goosebumps or just a sudden need to puke, you will recognize that feeling when you experience it and with practice, you will learn to trust it.

EMPLOY THE BEST PRACTICES IN ALL YOUR DEALINGS

Good, better, best.

Never let it rest.

Until your good is better and your better best.

St. Jerome

Christians have a saying, "you reap what you sow, "which is more than just a biblical phrase. It encapsulates the natural order of things. Of course, we know that bad things sometimes happen to very good people and vice versa. But, never believe for one moment that people do not get their retribution. Because they do. When you have been treated badly in life, you naturally want to shut yourself in and close yourself off to people. And if you have to deal with people, you want to always position yourself where you would have the upper hand. The problem with this kind of thinking is that because of your experiences, you become a victim who has made the decision [at least on a subconscious level] to make other people victims.

You may be able to find temporary pleasure in dealing the same card that other people have dealt you to innocent people but the damage in the long run can be devastating. Plus, you could end up setting off a chain of events with a domino effect that could come back to you. Even when you are presented with the opportunity, don't take it. Instead, turn the situation around by choosing to end the pain cycle with you. As someone who has been here, I can tell you that it is not easy. As a teenager, I was painfully shy. I found it difficult to talk to people. Even when I was with people like my parents and sibling, I still didn't crawl out of my shell entirely. But all that changed when I met Debbie. She was my high school dream, and I remember being painfully in love with her.

It took a lot of mental energy to finally work up the courage to ask her out on a date. And when I did, I was even more blown away by the fact that she said yes. I was walking on sunshine for the next 3 months until I found out that I was just a bet. Yes, I know it sounds remarkably like that teen movie that was a hit back in the day except this time, I was the victim. It hurt more than words can say, but that was not the worst part. I was humiliated the worst way a person like me can be. You know that dream we all have where you are standing on stage in front of the whole school and you suddenly find yourself naked? This was way worse than that.

I am not sure how I was able to get through that month in school much less the entire school year, but I did. Fast forward to my post-college years, I met Debbie again. Let us just say I was in a more advantageous position and I had the option of using my office to make her life difficult, but I chose not to. Initially, she interpreted this to mean I still had feelings for her, and she tried to work that to her advantage. I politely informed her that I was just doing my job. If I had held on to the feelings that I had for her in the past, I would have reacted differently. It was either she would have been successful in her attempts to seduce me or I would have been seduced into using the powers that my position offered to "punish" her. But I did neither. And in that decision, I found true freedom.

Life has a funny way of working itself out smoothly. Don't take it on yourself to be the dispenser of justice. Instead, arm yourself with the lessons learned, and use them to your advantage. Like St, Jerome said in the introductory quote, be your very best...even when you are put to the test.

CONCLUSION

I have heard people caution, "the heart of man is desperately wicked." I don't know who said it or where I heard it, but it stuck in my head, and I find it to be true. There are no devices or software applications that one can use to decipher the thoughts of another person. The best you can do is understand your own thoughts and feelings and do your best to live out your principles and values. But just because you can't tell if your new best friend is betraying or not should not mean you should spend your days obsessing over it.

Because yes, the true intentions of a man's heart are hidden. However, man's capacity to do good is equally as great as it is to go the other way, and this is not the best part. The best part is that for every single person who has hurt you in the past, there are a hundred more who want to do good by you. It may sound incredulous, but this is the reality of the situation. This book was not written to scare you into retreating into your shell and avoid dealing with people. On the contrary, I wrote it to help you make better choices in your relationships.

By understanding the tricks and tools that certain employ in their dealings with others, you are better equipped to protect yourself from such vices. And if you have been hurt by people, this book is meant to help you with the healing process. Nothing in life is ever concluded. We may have come to the end of the book, but it doesn't mean that your process has ended. If you take the lessons that I have shared with you to heart, you can successfully open yourself to the wonderful prospects life has in store for you. The journey to attaining a deeper understanding of self and discovering yourself on its own is a highly rewarding experience.

So, close this book, but keep your heart and mind open. Some of the clichés in life have a tremendous impact on our lives. Love hard, smile more, and most importantly, let go. Life is too precious and too wonderful to live it any other way. And always wake yourself up with the reminder that you deserve the best that life has to offer. Thank you for taking me on this journey with you!

Thank you

Before you go, I wanted to say "thank you" for purchasing my book.

You could have picked from dozens of other books on the same topic, but you took a chance and chose this one.

So, a HUGE thanks to you for getting this book and for reading all the way to the end.

Now I ask you for a small favor. Could you please consider posting a review on the platform? Reviews are one of the easiest ways to support the work of independent authors.

This feedback will help me continue to write the type of books that will help you get the results you want. So, if you enjoyed it, please let me know.

Lastly, don't forget to grab a copy of your Free Bonus book *"Bulletproof Confidence Checklist,"* If you want to learn how to overcome shyness, social anxiety, and become more confident, then this book is for you.

Just go to:
https://theartofmastery.com/confidence/